INSIGHT ⊙ GUIDES

EXPLORE

PRAGUE

◉ Walking Eye App

Your guide now includes a free eBook to your chosen destination, for the same great price as before. Simply download the Walking Eye App from the App Store or Google Play to access your free eBook.

HOW THE WALKING EYE APP WORKS

Through the Walking Eye App, you can purchase a range of eBooks and destination content. However, when you buy this book, you can download the corresponding eBook for free. Just see below in the grey panel where to find your free content and then scan the QR code at the bottom of this page.

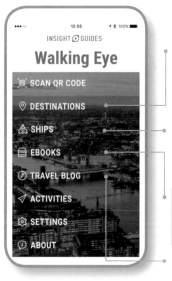

Destinations: Download essential destination content featuring recommended sights and attractions, restaurants, hotels and an A–Z of practical information, all available for purchase.

Ships: Interested in ship reviews? Find independent reviews of river and ocean ships in this section, all available for purchase.

ebooks: You can download your free accompanying digital version of this guide here. You will also find a whole range of other eBooks, all available for purchase.

Free access to travel-related blog articles about different destinations, updated on a daily basis.

HOW THE EBOOKS WORK

The eBooks are provided in EPUB file format. Please note that you will need an eBook reader installed on your device to open the file. Many devices come with this as standard, but you may still need to install one manually from Google Play.

The eBook content is identical to the content in the printed guide.

HOW TO DOWNLOAD THE WALKING EYE APP

1. Download the Walking Eye App from the App Store or Google Play.
2. Open the app and select the scanning function from the main menu.
3. Scan the QR code on this page – you will then be asked a security question to verify ownership of the book.
4. Once this has been verified, you will see your eBook in the purchased ebook section, where you will be able to download it.

Other destination apps and eBooks are available for purchase separately or are free with the purchase of the Insight Guide book.

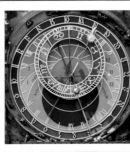

CONTENTS

ARCHITECTURE BUFFS

Wenceslas Square (route 8) displays the city's architectural styles, while Czech architecture (route 7), modern classics such as the 'Fred and Ginger' building in Nové Město (route 9) and Cubist designs (route 10) add to the mix.

RECOMMENDED ROUTES FOR...

ART ENTHUSIASTS

The city's major showcases for art include the National Gallery (route 2), the Strahov Collection of Art (route 3) and the Museum of Modern Art in the Functionalist Veletržní Palace (route 12).

CLASSIC CAFÉS

Take time out at a traditional café in the Old Town (route 5); check out such classic institutions as Café Slavia, Café Louvre and Café Imperial.

CHILDREN

Children can marvel at the albino peacocks and owls at the Waldstein Palace (route 4), ride on the Funicular Railway (route 3) and spend time at the zoo (route 13).

CZECH BEER

Those eager to check out the local brew should head for Smíchov (route 14), home to the famous Staropramen Brewery, which holds hour-long guided tours (with tastings).

HISTORY HUNTERS

Start at the Castle (route 1), then perhaps the Old Town (route 5) for its historic buildings, and Josefov (route 6), the city's Jewish Quarter. Further afield visit Vyšehrad (route 10), where it's said the city was founded.

MUSIC LOVERS

Follow in the footsteps of Smetana (route 5), Dvořák in Nové Město (route 9) and Mozart's music at the Estates Theatre (route 5). Opera buffs should head to the State Opera House (route 8).

PARKS AND GARDENS

The city's green spaces include the gardens of the Waldstein Palace (route 4), the University Botanical Gardens in Nové Město (route 9) and the Prague Botanical Garden (route 13).

INTRODUCTION

An introduction to Prague's geography, customs and culture, plus illuminating background information on cuisine, history and what to do when you're there.

Into Malá Strana

EXPLORE PRAGUE

Prague is one of the most beautiful and intriguing cities in Europe, justly famous for its Old Town and Castle. Yet beyond the crowds is another equally fascinating city – of galleries, gardens and iconic design.

Located at the heart of Europe, Prague ('Praha' in Czech) has been the capital of the ancient realm of Bohemia for centuries. During the Middle Ages it rose to prominence as the capital of Charles IV's vast empire. As Holy Roman Emperor and ruler of much of Western Europe, he was probably the most powerful man in the world at the time (1316–78).

In the late 16th and early 17th centuries the city was the seat of the Habsburg Court and it became the capital of the newly independent country of Czechoslovakia in 1918. After a *coup d'état* in 1948, Czechs chafed under the yoke of Communist rule; but when the Iron Curtain fell in 1989, it unveiled Prague's wealth of cultural treasures.

GEOGRAPHY AND LAYOUT

Prague used to be known as the 'Five Towns', and although it has now been divided into 10 separate districts, most visitors concentrate on the five historic towns: Hradčany; Staré Město (Old Town); Malá Strana (Lesser Quarter); Nové Město (New Town); and the former ghetto of the Jewish Quarter, known as Josefov. The city's administration was finally unified under the rule of Joseph II (1780–90), and the separate town halls are now merely reminders of previous autonomy.

In earlier times, the inhabitants of the congested Old Town and Jewish Quarter must have felt envious when they looked across to the New Town, where the far-sighted designs of Charles IV (1346–78) and his architects had created broad open spaces and avenues such as the Charles and Wenceslas squares. Today, however, the Old Town has been beautifully restored and the Jewish Quarter's Pařížská is a chic avenue lined with expensive shops.

The city's growth

As the city expanded (by the beginning of the 19th century, some 80,000 people lived here), further districts were added to the original five towns. The incorporation of Vyšehrad, Holešovice and Bubeneč brought the population to around 200,000 by 1900. After World War I, the city's area tripled to a size of 550 sq km (190 sq miles), and by 1930 the population had reached 850,000.

Under Communism, new suburbs such as Severní Město (North Town) and Jižní

The National Theatre

Trams are budget-friendly

Město (South Town) were built, and the expansion is ongoing. Today, the city has a population of over 1.3 million, while its wider metropolitan area is estimated to accommodate over 2 million people.

The Vltava River

As Prague's architecture envelops you in all its glory, you could be forgiven for overlooking one of the city's most beautiful sights: the Vltava River itself, its graceful S-shape unwinding in the heart of the city. A tributary of the Elbe, and at times going under its German name of Moldau, for centuries it has inspired writers and musicians alike – most notably the composer Bedřich Smetana (1824–84), whose symphonic poems dedicated to the river celebrate its lengthy journey across the Czech landscape on its way to Prague.

Architecture

Prague has one of the world's most pristine and varied cityscapes, encompassing Gothic, Renaissance, Baroque, neoclassical, Art Nouveau, Cubist and ultra-modern buildings. The centre of Prague is essentially a Gothic city with a Baroque face. Nearly all of its numerous churches were either built or remodelled during the Baroque period, and many of the original Gothic houses were given a new Baroque facade in the frenetic period of building and reconstruction initiated by the Habsburgs in the 17th century. And if the centre has a Baroque appearance, visitors who venture slightly further out might be surprised to find that Prague has some of the best examples of early 20th-century Modernist architecture of any European city.

The Communist years brought little in terms of *grands projets* to the city, but during the 1970s and 1980s, new suburbs of high-rise apartment blocks (the so-called *paneláky*) were built of pre-fabricated concrete panels. In contrast to the experience of similar projects elsewhere in Europe, Prague's new rent-controlled estates proved quite successful, developing strong communities and attracting tenants from across the social spectrum.

Climate

As a landlocked country in Central Europe, Prague tends to see continental weather patterns springing from Russia, but can also experience mild, wet weather from the Atlantic. Winters are on the whole cold and wet, but it can stay dry and clear for long spells. When the wind blows from Russia, it can be extremely cold. Summers are warm but rainy. June and July are two of the rainiest months of the year, while spring and autumn are marked by changeable weather. Bring a mac or umbrella just in case.

Getting around

The historic areas of Prague are compact, making them pleasurable to explore on foot – although the steep lanes or steps that lead up to Prague Castle do require a bit more exertion.

Prague's public transport infrastructure is very good and consists of an integrated transport system that includes the metro (three interconnecting lines), a tram system (31 tram routes), buses, the Petřín funicular and six ferry lines. All services have a common ticketing system, and, in comparison with public transport in many other European cities, prices are surprisingly inexpensive. Taxis are always available but can be a pricey option; choose with care.

Flooding

In August 2002, floods threatened to do more damage to Prague's historic fabric than centuries of political upheavals. Sewers overflowed and submerged the streets in stinking muck. Streets buckled and buildings collapsed. Metro stations were flooded to street level. At Prague Zoo, a gorilla was drowned and an elephant and a hippo had to be shot when they could not be rescued. Fortunately, the clean-up and restoration programme went surprisingly smoothly, and today there are few remaining signs that the flooding ever took place. Praguers have always lived with the constant threat of flooding when excessive rainfall swells the Vltava and the streets were once again under water in 2013. Some metro stations were closed and people evacuated. However with millions of crowns of investment in flood defences following the 2002 disaster, the damage was not as severe. Even the lowest barriers are some 30cm higher than the highest flood level in 2002 and with further removable barriers and pumps the city authorities hope such a disaster will never happen again. The city, however, with the mighty Vltava River at its heart will ultimately be at the mercy of the weather.

LIFE SINCE THE VELVET REVOLUTION

There have, of course, been many changes since the Velvet Revolution of 1989 for both the city and its people. Although the optimism that followed the revolution has now died down – not least as the Czechs face up to life under capitalism, membership of the European Union (EU) and Nato, and a string of corruption scandals – there is still a sense that the city is rediscovering and reinventing its past.

Sense of identity

Some complain that city life now seems bland and somehow less vital. Feelings inherent in life in one of the smaller EU member states – a sense of powerlessness, that the action is taking place elsewhere – stand in stark contrast to the idealism and activism of intellectual life under the tyranny of Communism. Prague's days as a European centre of writers and artists have all but vanished too. Meanwhile, the younger generation has grown up with the kinds of freedoms long taken for granted by teenagers in

Christmas market on the Old Town Square

the West, and, naturally enough, has used them to embrace consumerism.

Much, however, has been preserved. Praguers are still able to enjoy the city's architectural heritage, and it was fortunate to suffer considerably less damage during World War II than many other major European cities (with only a few bombing raids by the US Air Force towards the end of the war).

Prosperity

The last couple of decades have also brought prosperity to the Czech Republic in general, and Prague in particular. The Czech economy has grown contin-

---

DON'T LEAVE PRAGUE WITHOUT ...

Ambling the labyrinth of lanes that is Staré Město. You'll discover superb historic buildings, plus interesting little shops that radiate off the beautiful Old Town Square. Be sure to catch the Astronomical Clock as it comes to life every hour on the hour. See page 48.

Crossing the Charles Bridge as the sun rises. While it's still free from tourists, explore the canals under the bridge known as Prague's 'Little Venice'. Then climb the Old Town Bridge Tower for a bird's-eye view. See page 40.

Admiring the view from the Garden of the Ramparts at Prague Castle. The garden's central terrace offers a breathtaking view over the city. Then further explore the Castle complex, including the pretty Golden Lane and St Vitus's Cathedral. See page 28.

Exploring Wenceslas Square for an insight into Czech history. This important landmark has witnessed events from the proclamation of independence to the Velvet Revolution. See page 66.

Following in the footsteps of Franz Kafka. Pay homage to the writer among the cobbled streets of Josefov, Prague's Jewish Quarter. Visit the synagogues and a historic cemetery here, and the Franz Kafka Museum across the river. See page 56.

Taking coffee at one of the city's historic cafés. The coffee house was one of the great institutions of the interwar First Republic. Seek out the Art Deco Café Slavia – once packed with poets, artists and actors – and still very much in business. See page 111.

Taking the little funicular to the top of Petřín Hill. From here you can enjoy countrified views and climb even higher by taking the 299 steps up the Observation Tower. See page 38.

Riding the nostalgic tram No. 91. This old tram runs along a city-centre route from the Transport Museum, taking in a number of sights. The trip (every weekend Apr – mid-Nov) takes about 40 minutes, leaving on the hour. See page 130.

Boarding a steamboat for a cruise down the Vltava. A river cruise is a fascinating way to see Prague's diverse architecture from a different perspective. Floating under Charles Bridge, you can fully appreciate what a work of art it is. See page 128.

ually since 1999, and from the second quarter of 2005 to mid-2008, the rate of growth did not fall below 6 percent. Since then, the country has weathered the world financial downturn far better than many of its European neighbours, thanks to relatively low levels of public debt (30–40 percent of GDP), a stable banking sector, and the fact that over 99 percent of household debts were denominated in the local Czech currency. Even so, exports (particularly to Germany) did suffer a decline and the economy contracted in 2009 – though has since recovered well. Plans for the Czech Republic to join the Eurozone have repeatedly been put back due to opposition from the public; according to a 2016 poll 78 percent of Czechs were against joining, and there is no target date for adopting the euro.

Prague itself has become the location of the European headquarters of many international companies, while its manufacturing industries – including textiles, engineering and brewing – have survived the transition to the free market. However, the city's architectural heritage has also brought a new industry that dwarfs the old: most of the city's income now derives from tourism. This in turn has allowed historic buildings to benefit from a massive renovation programme and important new buildings to be commissioned from the likes of architects Frank Gehry and Jean Nouvel.

On an individual level, capitalist economics have also brought relative wealth. While unemployment nationally is running at approximately 4.5 percent (the lowest in the EU), in Prague it stands at virtually zero. Moreover, income is much higher than in other parts of the country. Even so, the prices charged in tourist restaurants and cafés make the centre of Prague expensive for most of the capital's citizens.

With more disposable cash from an improved economy, prosperous Praguers are starting to assert their purchasing power. Shiny shopping malls that house many well-known Western European stores tempt them to spend their hard-earned cash. Once mainly the prerogative of visitors, chic contemporary hotels and adventurous fusion restaurants are now very much on their agenda, and bars and cafés are brimming over with trendy young locals.

Without doubt tourism has taken over from industry as the city's big earner and visitors to Prague are pampered more than ever before. The city is a cultural hotspot: choose from a plethora of classical music – staged in stunning concert halls and an array of beautiful churches, palaces and historic buildings – to a rich repertoire of opera and ballet. Innovative Black Light theatre thrills audiences while Prague's nightlife scene is flourishing. All this coupled with a boom in four- and five-star hotels, a growing choice of eating and drinking options and newly renovated museums Prague has most certainly arrived as a main contender in the tourism stakes.

The Charles Bridge spans the Vltava River

TOP TIPS FOR EXPLORING PRAGUE

Markets. Consider making a December trip to Prague when the Old Town Square twinkles with thousands of lights and the Christmas Market stalls showcase local products and mulled wine.

Towers with a view. Get up high for fantastic panoramic views round the city. Climb the Old Town Hall and Old Town Bridge towers or the tower of the Church of St Nicholas, where you also get a close-up of the church's dome and statuary.

Classical concerts. Sublime classical music concerts are performed in churches and historic buildings across Prague; check out www.pragueclassicalconcerts. com for an amazing variety of atmospheric venues.

Steamboat to the zoo. Combine a cruise with a trip to the zoo and the Troja Château. The Prague Steamboat Company (PPS; www.praguesteamboats.com) runs a service (March to October) from Raišín Embankment or Čech Bridge to Císařký Island near the palace, which is opposite the zoo.

Křivoklát. A trip out of the city to Karlštejn can easily be combined with a visit to the spectacular Gothic castle at Křivoklát about 40 minutes further along the same railway line beyond Beroun. Křivoklát, set in the forest, is usually much less crowded than Karlštejn.

Traditional beer halls. First-timers should try these: U Fleků, Křemencova 11, a legendary watering hole; U Vejvodů, Jilská 4, done out as a Bohemian alehouse; U Zlatého Tygra, Husova 17, good value and popular with locals; U Medvídků, Na Perštýně 7, pace yourself for the 11.8 percent X Beer 33.

Souvenirs. The shops at The House of the Black Madonna, Kubista and Modernista sell reproduction Cubist designs (albeit expensive). Glassware is synonymous with the Czech Republic, for good quality try Moser at Staroměstské náměstí, or for more contemporary styles Artěl at Celetná 29.

Places of worship. Although dress code in churches is fairly relaxed in Prague men should cover their heads in both Jewish synagogues and cemeteries; paper *yarmulkes* are available, but a hat or bandana will do.

Multiple National Gallery sites. The collections of Prague's National Gallery are spread out over several different sites: European art is in the Sternberg Palace; Bohemian Baroque art is held opposite in the Schwarzenberg Palace and 19th-century art is displayed in Salm Palace next door; medieval art of Central Europe is found at the Convent of St Agnes; the Kinský Palace largely displays Asian art; and modern art can be seen in the Trade Fair Palace.

Changing of the guard. Prague Castle is the official residence and office of the President of the Czech Republic, and at noon you can see the 'Changing of the Guard' in the first courtyard of the castle. The formal handover is carried out with a fanfare and flag ceremony. Arrive early to find a good spot to see the parade.

Sizzling sausages

FOOD AND DRINK

Czech food tends to the hearty and comforting end of the culinary spectrum, with a great emphasis on pork and dumplings; for those with a good appetite, it is wonderful. Even better, perhaps, is the country's delicious beer.

Bohemian cooking is based on the abundant produce of the country's fertile farmland, its orchards, rivers and ponds, and its vast forests teeming with game. It is unpretentious fare, intended to sustain body and soul rather than form the subject of sophisticated conversation. Nonetheless, it can be delicious.

WHAT TO EAT

Breakfast
The Czechs begin the day in a frugal way, with a breakfast (*snídaně*) often consisting of only a cup of coffee (*káva*) – perhaps still made in the time-honoured fashion by pouring boiling water onto finely ground beans in the cup and letting the mixture settle before attempting to drink it.

Food on the move
Once out and about, the Praguer's appetite is likely to be whetted by the sight of one of the city's many sausage stands. Czech sausages are among the best in the world. The favourite is the *párek* (often sold in pairs as *párky*) – a Frankfurter that should really be called a Praguer as it was from here that it originated. A fatter version is called a *vuřt* (*cf.* German *Wurst*), while a *klobása* is an even bigger specimen – coarse-textured, with a thick skin and plenty of fatty globules. Whichever your sausage of choice, it is customary to adorn it with a dollop of mild mustard.

Marginally healthier snacks are available in the form of little open sandwiches (*obložené chlebíčky*), bought at delicatessens. Toppings may include slivers of ham, salami, hard-boiled egg, fish roe, potato salad, slices of tomato and gherkins.

Lunch
A full Czech lunch (*oběd*) will normally begin with soup (*polévka*), whether a simple meat broth (*vývar*) with dumplings, a thick potato cream soup (*bramborová*) or a bowl of tripe soup (*dršťková* – reputed to be an excellent hangover cure).

The main course is referred to half-jokingly as *vepřo-knedlo-zelo* (pork-dumpling-cabbage). Indeed, the pig is king in this country: every part is made into some tasty comestible. After pork, beef (*hovězí maso*) is the most popular meat, and is often served as *svíčková na smetaně*, fillet or sirloin topped with a slice of lemon and a spoonful of cran-

Roast duck and dumplings

The ever-popular goulash

berries, and swimming in a cream sauce. Other main courses at lunchtime might include veal *(telecí maso)* or chicken *(kuře)*. Also particularly popular is the paprika-laced goulash *(guláš)*.

The usual accompaniment to meat is the dumpling *(knedlík)* – which, in fact, enjoys even more veneration than the pig. It is made from flour, bread, potatoes or semolina, with added yeast, baking powder, eggs, milk or sugar, and is prepared in a loaf-like form and then cut with a wire (never a knife).

When it comes to vegetables, cabbage is the most popular. Salad *(salát)* is more common, probably not in the form of tossed green leaves, but as a medley of cucumber, onion, red pepper and tomatoes wallowing in a sweetish, vinegary sauce.

As for dessert, options are limited. There may be thin crêpes *(palačinky)* wrapped around cottage cheese *(tvaroh)*, ice cream *(zmrzlina)*, fruit or nuts, perhaps served with a chocolate sauce. The dumpling makes a reappearance (like it or not), this time as an *ovocný knedlík*, filled with plums or apricots.

Cakes and pastries

Any disappointment over dessert may easily be alleviated in Prague's cafés *(kavárna)* and patisseries *(cukrárna)*. Here, you are spoilt for choice: tarts, strudels, sponge cakes, éclairs and *kolíčky* – buns filled with *tvaroh* (poppy seeds) or *povidla* (a delicious, dense, dark plum jam).

Dinner

Dinner is the moment to move beyond *vepřo-knedlo-zelo* and sample richer dishes such as roast duck *(kachna)* or even better, roast goose *(husa)*. As well as making a celebratory meal for grand occasions, geese in the Czech Republic are also force-fed to provide *husí paštíka*, liver pâté as good as the finest French *foie gras* (irresistible, as long as you don't dwell on what the unfortunate bird has had to go through).

Some restaurants also offer an opportunity to sample the excellent variety of game reared in the fields and forests beyond Bohemia's villages. Look out for dishes featuring wild boar *(kanec)*, venison *(srnčí maso)*, pheasant *(bažant)* or partridge *(koroptev)*.

As regards fish, Prague is a landlocked country a long way from the ocean, so it makes sense to try the freshwater kind. Roasted or fried trout *(pstruh)* features on many menus, but the quintessentially Czech fish is the carp *(kapr)*. Carp are raised in their thousands in fishponds across the country. In restaurants, carp is more likely to be served as *kapr na černo* in a black, sweet-and-sour sauce made mysteriously from ingredients that include nuts, raisins, sugar, beer and vinegar.

VEGETARIANS

Vegetarians will find specialist establishments catering to their needs, which is just as well since mainstream restau-

Czech beer

Although the oldest record of the brewer's art in Prague can be found in a document dating from 1082, the bottom-fermented Czech beers of today have evolved from the brew developed in the western Bohemian city of Plzeň (Pilsen) in 1842. The combination of local spring water, hops from Žatec in northern Bohemia, and cellaring in the ideal conditions of the sandstone caves beneath the city yielded a beer that won instant popularity – particularly in Germany, where its name, 'Pilsner' or 'Pils', is now indiscriminately applied to any pale, hoppy brew. To distinguish the original product from its imitators, its makers gave it the name of 'Pilsner Urquell' meaning 'original source' (*Plzeňský prazdroj'* in Czech). Its great rival is Budčjovice – known as Budweis in German and Budvar in Czech – which comes from the southern city of České Budějovice. For those who find the distinctive sharp taste of Prazdroj a little too acidic, Budvar is a somewhat sweeter, milder drink.

Most Czech beer is of the Pilsner type, and is referred to as *svetlé* (light). It comes in two strengths, measured in degrees – indicating the amount of sugar content. What is described as '12°' *(dvánactka)* is stronger and heavier, with an alcohol content of over 4 percent; '10°' *(desetka)* is lighter and contains less than 4 percent alcohol. As well as *svelté*, most breweries also make *tmavé*, a dark and rather sweet beer not unlike British mild. It is sometimes cut with *svelté* in order to combine the advantages of both.

rants are unlikely to offer them much more than an omelette or fried cheese *(smážený sýr)*; the latter is better than it sounds, consisting of a thick slice of semi-molten local cheese (usually *hermelín*) in a breadcrumb coating and enlivened by a tasty dollop of tartare sauce.

Fungi of various descriptions may also be on offer in Prague. The environment of the Czech Republic is particularly favourable for the growth of a bewildering array of mushrooms *(houby)*, a detailed knowledge of which seems part of everyone's heritage. Fungi in all shapes and sizes are hunted down and picked in favourite spots in the countryside, brought home and fried or more likely dried, to be added later to all kinds of dishes, notably cabbage soup.

WHERE TO EAT AND DRINK

Prague restaurants *(restaurace)* vary enormously in character and price. The city still retains a strong traditional culinary presence despite the increasing number of good international restaurants and eating out is good-value by western European standards. Michelin stars are emerging as talented chefs take on the local cuisine and add their own innovative touches. Currently Prague has three Michelin-star restaurants: Alcron Hotel (see page 114); Field (www.fieldrestaurant.cz) and La Dégustation (see page 112).

The Art Nouveau interior of Café Imperial, a Prague institution since 1914

Pubs and bars

The most basic establishment is the *hostinec* or *pivnice* (beer house), a simple watering hole that serves basic food.

Next up the ladder is the *hospoda*, the pub or beer hall. Most pubs are tied to a particular brewery, serving its product on draught in half-litre glasses. Some take great pride in the way in which they keep and serve their beer; the reputation of U zlatého Tygra (The Golden Tiger; www.uzlatehotygra.cz), a well-known pub in the Old Town, is largely based on the temperature of its ancient cellars, which is ideal for the perfect preservation of Pilsner.

Many *hospody* serve perfectly good meals (perhaps with a more limited choice), and those at the top end of the scale may be very similar to *restaurace*.

Coffee houses

The coffee house was one of the great institutions of the interwar First Republic. Some have faded into history – for example, the Arco, meeting place of 'Arconauts' Franz Kafka, Franz Werfel and Max Brod. Others are still in business, such as the Café Slavia (see page 111) filled in its heyday with poets, painters, and actors from the National Theatre opposite.

DRINKS

The Czech Republic is home to what many consider the world's finest beers, but it is also wine country, and in addition produces a number of unusual spirits and aperitifs.

Winemaking in the Czech Republic is concentrated in sunny southern Moravia, where the vines spread for 115km (70 miles) between the city of Brno and the Austrian and Slovak borders. Among the red wines, Frankovka (dry) or Sv. Vavřinec (plummy and sweet) can be good, while white *Ryzlink* and *Palava* go well with fish.

Bohemia's vineyards cover a much smaller area, centred on the Elbe and its tributaries north of Prague. The vines growing on the steep slope below the town of Mělník are the descendants of those brought from France and planted here by Emperor Charles IV in the 14th century. They yield white wines that are dry and acidic, like those in neighbouring Saxony.

More or less palatable fruit brandies are also distilled. The best is probably Slivovice, made from plums, though you may also try apricot brandy, *meruňkovice*, and cherry brandy, *třešňovice*. The most popular aperitif is Becherovka, a liquor originally served as a restorative to Karlsbad spa guests, and made from a secret herbal recipe. Finally, the Czech Republic is one of the few countries where absinthe is legally made and consumed.

Bohemian glass

SHOPPING

Prague is not an international shopping destination like London, Paris or New York, but aside from the same chains and shiny Western-style shopping malls you find everywhere there are some interesting local shops.

The centre of Prague is increasingly given over to shiny new shopping centres, which are full of international high-street chains. In addition large malls now ring the city centre. A sizeable number of international designers have set up shop along the posher avenues, but a number of Czech designers have made their mark. Service has improved markedly since the early post-Communist days of grumpy state-employed assistants who seemed to resent your presence in their establishments.

SHOPPING AREAS

The best shopping is generally to be found in Staré and Nové Město, although some of the outlying districts now have huge shopping centres. The main commercial streets of central Prague, with dependably long hours all year round, are Wenceslas Square (Václavské náměstí) and Na příkopě. If you are looking for expensive international fashion then head for Pařížská, which runs off Old Town Square.

Some of the small streets in the Old Town, such as V Kolkovně, Dušní, Týnská and Panská, have a number of exciting and unusual boutiques. The Týn Court-yard near Old Town Square also has numerous little shops that are worth exploring, as do the backstreets of Malá Strana. If you are looking for a department store try either Kotva on náměstí Republiky, or Marks and Spencer in the Palladium shopping centre opposite.

WHAT TO BUY

Czech souvenirs

There are a number of locally produced items that are worth looking out for. You will not be able to avoid Bohemian glass and china, held in high esteem throughout the world because of their quality and value for money. New items from major manufacturers are still excellent (try Moser at Staroměstské náměstí, or for more contemporary styles Artěl at Celetná 29), but now it's almost impossible to find a good deal in antiques shops. Antiques dealers have become wise to the foreign market for their wares and have altered their prices accordingly.

If you're looking for something typically Bohemian to take home as a gift, a bottle of the herbal liqueur Becherovka or some Slivovice is a good idea. Fruity wines from Bohemia and Moravia will also be appre-

Designer ceramics at Kubista

ciated. Wooden toys and marionettes make excellent gift items for children. These can be found in Obchod Loutkami at Nerudova 47.

Street vendors – concentrated in Hradčany and on the Charles Bridge – sell handmade goods, such as marionettes and costume jewellery, as well as items of dubious use and value, such as refrigerator magnets depicting famous Prague sights.

Music

Classical music CDs, especially those of Czech music from the record label Supraphon, are cheaper than in the UK or US. The performances, by superb Czech ensembles and musicians, are always good and often thrilling. Also look out for recordings by local jazz and experimental rock musicians. One of the best places to find classical and contemporary music is the large Bontonland Megastore in the basement of the Koruna Building on the corner of Wenceslas Square. A good range of classical CDs can also be found at Via Musica on Staroměstské námestí.

Fashion

Although Prague seems overwhelmed by international chains and designers, local fashion by Prague designers can be found and their clothes are often interesting and well made. In the Old Town there are a number of interesting places. Klára Nademlýnská's sexy and fashionable clothes can be had at Dlouhá 3,

while, nextdoor but sharing the same address, Beáta Rajská embodies elegance in her luxury designs. One of the most interesting places is Hard-de-Core (Senovážné námestí 10), the brainchild of inspired designers Josefina Bakošová and Petra Krčková. This is not just a fashion shop but an institution stocking jewellery, ceramics and other handmade designs not to be found anywhere else. The owners will also design your party decorations and are happy to teach you some of their skills.

Design duo

Kubista and Modernista are not only two of the most chic design boutiques in Prague but they also offer some of the best and most unusual souvenirs of your visit. Both capitalise on Prague's extraordinary outpouring of cutting-edge design during the first half of the 20th century. The first (Ovocný trh 19; tel: 224 236 378; www.kubista.cz; Tue–Sun 10am–6pm), not surprisingly, concentrates on superb reproductions of Czech Cubist works, including ceramics and furniture, as well as selling a number of original pieces. Fittingly, it is located in the Cubist House of the Black Madonna, as is Modernista (tel: 224 241 300; www.modernista.cz; Tue–Sun 10am–6pm), which by contrast, concentrates on slightly later works with reproductions of pieces by Adolf Loos and Functionalist designers.

Black Light theatre performance at Laterna magika

ENTERTAINMENT

While Prague is justly famous for its classical music ensembles – from opera at the National Theatre to the Czech Philharmonic at the Rudolfinum – there is much more on offer, including jazz, theatre and film.

Prague can rival any other capital city in Europe when it comes to choice in entertainment. There really is something for every taste from the vibrant cultural scene both in classical and modern performance to cocktail bars and clubs, traditional Czech folklore evenings and opera to beer tastings and river dinner cruises.

MUSIC

Concerts of classical music, mainly chamber ensembles, are held in churches and historic buildings across the city. Some are aimed solely at tourists; the standard is not always particularly high, and the repertory is fairly predictable. There are also, however, some exceptional venues, putting on some of the best concerts to be heard anywhere.

The Czech Philharmonic is one of the world's great orchestras, and seeing one of its concerts at the Rudolfinum is a real event. The city's other major resident orchestra is the Prague Symphony Orchestra. Less well known than the Czech Philharmonic but still excellent, it performs its concerts in the splendid Obecní dům (see page 64) from September to June. A third orchestra, the Prague Radio

Symphony Orchestra, is also resident in the city. Although primarily a recording ensemble for Czech Radio, it puts on a fine concert series in the Rudolfinum between October and March. It is an outstanding orchestra, often including contemporary works in its programmes.

One of the most high-profile chamber ensembles is the Suk Chamber Orchestra, founded in 1974 by world-renowned violinist Josef Suk (1929–2011; grandson of the famous composer of the same name). It tends to concentrate on the core Czech repertory. Two orchestras established since 1989 and starting to make an international name for themselves are the Prague Philharmonia and the Czech National Symphony Orchestra.

Opera and ballet

The quality of opera in Prague is high. Most opera is sung in its original language with digital surtitles in Czech. (Performances of works by Czech composers such as Dvořák and Smetana do not have surtitles in foreign languages.)

The National Theatre Ballet frequently performs classics such as *Swan Lake* and *Coppélia*, but has been branching out in more adventurous directions in

National Theatre play   *Exquisite lines at the National Ballet*

recent years by including choreographies by George Balanchine and Jiří Kylián. The Prague State Opera Ballet is a medium-sized company, which incorporated the Prague Chamber Ballet in 2003.

Jazz

Prague has a lively and very well-established jazz scene, with a number of decent clubs that at times attract big-name foreign artists. However, there are also several excellent local players who can be seen nightly at the city's clubs – notably bass-player Robert Balzar, jazz pianist Emil Viklický and guitarist Luboš Andršt.

THEATRE

Theatre in Prague has a long and venerable tradition – as might be expected in the capital of a country that, in 1989, chose a playwright as its first post-Communist president. There is still a lively theatrical scene in Prague, but, unless you are fluent in Czech, little will be accessible.

Probably of more interest to non-Czech speakers – and to children – are Prague's puppet theatres and the so-called 'Black Light' theatre developed for the 1958 World Expo. The most popular puppet show uses Josef Skupka's time-honoured characters of Spejbl and his son Hurvínek, and there are avant-garde, highly original performances too. A good place to watch a performance is the National Marionette Theatre (Žatecká 1; www.mozart.cz).

During performances of Black Light theatre – the most famous company is

at the Laterna magika – films and slides are projected onto multiple screens while actors, dressed completely in black to render them invisible, perform on stage, accompanied by a clever play of coloured lights. A certain amount of acrobatic skill is also often required of the actors.

FILM

There is a long tradition of Czech film in a variety of genre (see page 135) and annual film festivals are popular. There are several Cinema City multiplexes throughout Prague showing films in English: the most central in Na Příkopě on the southern edge of the Old Town. For art-house cinema try Kino Aero at Biskupcova 31 where many screenings are in English.

NIGHTLIFE

Prague is not a leading centre of nightlife in the way that London or Berlin are, but it still endeavours to hold its own against smaller European capital cities. Generally, it's a good idea to avoid the places in the Wenceslas Square area, which tend to attract either mobs of teenage tourists or a rather seedy crowd; most local people don't go there. The better clubs can be found sprinkled all over the city, and there is no single best area for nightlife. Clubs usually start around 11pm and stay open until 4am; some stay open later. Up-to-date nightlife listings can be found on the Czech-language site www.techno.cz. Further listings can be found on www.expats.cz.

Prague circa 1572

HISTORY: KEY DATES

From the early Přemyslids to the Hussites and Habsburgs, through the early Republic, Fascism, Communism and then into the EU, Prague's history is long and complex, and has built the fascinating mix that is the contemporary city.

EARLY PERIOD TO THE PŘEMYSLID DYNASTY

c.400 BC	Invasion by the Celtic Boii, from whom 'Bohemia' is derived.
AD 500s	Arrival of the Slavs.
900–1306	Rule of the Přemyslid dynasty; building of Prague Castle.
935	Prince Wenceslas, patron saint of Bohemia, is murdered by his brother Boleslav I.
1004	Bohemia comes under the jurisdiction of the Holy Roman Empire as Jaromír of Bohemia takes Prague with the aid of a German army.
1306	King Wenceslas II is assassinated, ending the Přemyslid dynasty.

THE GOLDEN AGE TO THE HUSSITE WARS

1310	King John of Luxembourg begins a new dynasty.
1348–78	Reign of King Charles I (later Emperor Charles IV); Charles Bridge built.
1398–1415	Jan Hus preaches religious reform and is burnt at the stake.
1419	The 'first defenestration of Prague' (see box page 44) begins the Hussite Wars, which continue intermittently for a century.

HABSBURG RULE

1526	Jagiellon King Louis is killed; the throne passes to the Habsburgs.
1576	Emperor Rudolf II moves the Habsburg court to Prague.
1609	Rudolf's Letter of Majesty grants freedom of religious worship.
1618	Archduke Ferdinand tears up the Letter of Majesty. The 'second defenestration of Prague' prompts the Thirty Years' War.
1620	Repression against Protestants results in mass exile.
1680	Bohemian peasants revolt against the feudal government.
1740	War of the Austrian Succession: the armies of Bavaria, Saxony and France capture Prague. Maria Theresa becomes empress.

Velvet Revolution protest in Prague

1757	Seven Years' War: Prussian forces bombard Prague. Maria Theresa has the castle extended and the damage to the city repaired.
1781	Joseph II abolishes serfdom; Prague's Jewish citizens are awarded civic rights. The ghetto is renamed Josefov.
1845	Arrival of the railway. The Industrial Revolution draws in Czechs from the countryside, diluting the German character of the city.
1848	Nationalist revolution in Prague crushed by the Austrians.
1880s	The Czech National Theatre opens. Composers Smetana, Dvořák and, later, Janáček gain international recognition.

INDEPENDENCE, THEN FASCISM, THEN COMMUNISM

1915	Tomáš Garrigue Masaryk goes into exile and gains Allied support for a new state uniting Czechs and Slovaks.
1918	Independent Republic of Czechoslovakia proclaimed. Masaryk becomes the first president, Edvard Beneš Foreign Minister.
1938	Munich Agreement cedes the Sudetenland to Hitler.
1939–45	Nazi occupation.
1945	Prague liberated by the Resistance and the Red Army. Almost all of Czechoslovakia's 2.7 million Germans are expelled.
1948	Communist coup replaces President Beneš with Klement Gottwald.
1968	Prague Spring: an attempt to introduce 'socialism with a human face' under Party Secretary General Alexander Dubček. Attempt is crushed by a Warsaw Pact invasion.
1969	Dubček dismissed and 'normalisation' – a return to Stalinist orthodoxy – is overseen by party leader Gustav Husák.

THE POST-COMMUNIST ERA

1989	The 'Velvet Revolution' ends the Communist era. Václav Havel is elected president.
1993	The 'Velvet Divorce' creates separate Czech and Slovak republics.
2002	Prague suffers severe flooding.
2003	Havel is succeeded as president by Václav Klaus.
2004	The Czech Republic joins the European Union (EU).
2011	Václav Havel dies in December and is given a state funeral.
2014	The city elects its first female mayor, Adriana Krnáčová.
2017	Czech legislative elections in October.

BEST ROUTES

St Vitus's Cathedral and the Castle

PRAGUE CASTLE

The history of Prague began with the construction of the castle in the 9th century. Its attractive mix of palaces, churches, museums, streets, gardens and galleries gives a fascinating insight into the origins of the city.

DISTANCE: 1km (0.75 mile)
TIME: A full day
START: Malostranská metro station
END: Belvedere
POINTS TO NOTE: Although this route only covers a short distance, there is a lot to pack in, as it includes many of Prague's top sights. As one of Europe's major tourist attractions Prague Castle is busy year-round, but try to avoid the weekend crowds, especially in summer.

Prague Castle, or Pražský hrad (www. hrad.cz; for opening times see box on page 30), sprawls across the district known as Hradčany. Set on a hill overlooking the city, it is Prague's most impressive sight, especially when illuminated at night. More than 1,000 years old, it was the residence of the early Přemyslid rulers, who did well to establish their headquarters in this strategic position over the Vltava. Generations of rulers continued to expand the complex with churches and pal-

aces, defensive and residential buildings. It is also the centre of spiritual power in the city, as the site of the cathedral of St Vitus, and it retains its link with temporal power as the residence of the president of the Czech Republic.

Emblem at Prague Castle   *Guarding the Castle*

OLD CASTLE STEPS

Begin at Malostranská metro station or the neighbouring tram stop. Turn left out of the station and walk up the hill, crossing Valdštejnská. This brings you to the bottom of the Old Castle Steps.

Lobkowicz Palace

The steep climb brings you up to the **Black Tower ❶** (Černá věž) entrance to the castle. Through the gate on the left is the entrance to the **Lobkowicz Palace ❷** (Lobkovický palác; www.lobkowicz.cz; daily 10am–6pm). Previously in the hands of the state, this building was returned to the Lobkowicz family and is now home to their private art collection. The star exhibit is Pieter Brueghel the Elder's *Haymaking*, but there are also manuscripts by Mozart and Beethoven as well as a display of armour.

Golden Lane

Further up Jiřská and to the right is the entrance to the attractive **Golden Lane ❸** (Zlatá ulička), one of the most popular attractions of the castle. It is said that Rudolf II housed his alchemists in these tiny houses, and Franz Kafka lived for a while at No. 22. At the end of the lane is the **Dalibor Tower ❹** (Daliborka), part of the castle wall.

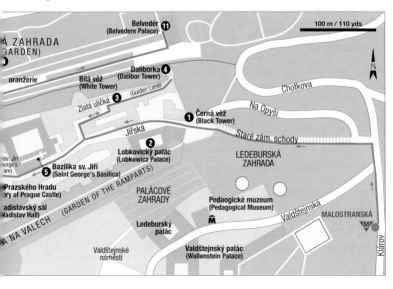

Golden Lane

St George's Basilica

Jiřská ends at Náměstí sv. Jiří (St George's Square). To the right is **St George's Basilica** 5 (Bazilika sv. Jiří), the oldest church still standing in the castle complex. It was founded around AD 920 and rebuilt after a fire in the 12th century. Despite later alterations, the church has largely retained its Romanesque appearance. To the right of the choir is the Ludmilla Chapel, housing the tomb of the saint, the grandmother of Prince Wenceslas.

The church was part of a large monastic complex and the convent next door now house short-term art exhibitions.

OLD ROYAL PALACE

Dominating Náměstí sv. Jiří is the large bulk of St Vitus's Cathedral. However, ignore this for the moment and pass through the arch between the church and buildings to the left, and turn sharp left to the **Old Royal Palace** 6 (Starý královský palác).

An anteroom opens on to the **Vladislav Hall** (Vladislavský sál), named after King Vladislav II. This imposing late Gothic throne room was built by the architect Benedikt Ried between 1493 and 1502.

On the same level, to the right, is the Bohemian Chancellery. It was from here that the imperial ambassadors were 'defenestrated' in 1618 (see page 44), sparking off the Thirty Years' War. At the far end of the Vladislav Hall is a balcony overlooking the interior of All Saints' Chapel, and the staircase that leads up from a doorway in the left-hand

wall of the hall brings you to the New Land Records Office. This is decorated with the heraldic emblems of the Land Rolls officials on the ceiling and walls. The exit to the palace rooms takes you down the Riders' Staircase, built to allow rulers and guests to enter on horseback.

The lowest Gothic levels of the palace are now home to **The Story of Prague Castle**. This informative display is particularly good for children; the first part leads from room to room describing the development of the castle in chronological order; the second tells the 'Story of …' various subjects, including learning, burials, the Church and patronage.

The Basilica of St George   *Basilica of St George door detail*

ST VITUS

Continue around the cathedral to the main entrance at its western end. Founded in 1344, **St Vitus's Cathedral** ❼ (Katedrála sv. Víta; Apr–Oct Mon–Sat 9am–5pm, Sun noon–5pm, Nov–Mar Mon–Sat 9am–4pm, Sun noon–4pm; vestibule free) is the largest church in Prague, the metropolitan church of the Archdiocese of Prague, the royal and imperial burial church and also the place where the royal regalia are kept. Charles IV employed French Gothic architect Matthew of Arras and, when he died, Petr Parléř took over. Work was halted in the first half of the 15th century by the Hussite Wars. In the 1860s, a Czech patriotic association, using the old plans, resumed building, finishing in 1929.

Wenceslas Chapel
Aside from the superb vaulting in Parléř's splendid nave, the highlight is the **Wenceslas Chapel**. Built by Parléř on the south transept, it is where the national saint Wenceslas was buried; the walls are covered with frescoes and precious stones. A little door leads up to the Treasure Chamber where the Bohemian royal regalia are kept, behind seven locks (the seven keys are held by seven separate institutions).

PICTURE GALLERY

Leave the cathedral and walk through the archway opposite to the Second Courtyard of the castle. If in need of refreshment, turn left and take the archway out over the bridge (Prašný most): a little further on is restaurant **Lví Dvůr**, see ❶.

After eating, retrace your steps to the entrance to the Second Courtyard. On your right is the **Prague Castle Picture Gallery** ❽ (Obrazárna Pražského hradu). This small but valuable collection was put together by Rudolf II, and although it has been plundered over the years, it still includes notable works by Rubens, Tintoretto, Titian and Veronese. Across the courtyard the Chapel of the Holy Cross protrudes, which holds the **Treasury of St Vitus Cathedral** exhibition (daily 10am–6pm).

ROYAL GARDEN AND BELVEDERE

Cross back over the bridge then turn right into the **Royal Garden** ❾ (Královská zahrada; 10am–6pm), home to two important Renaissance buildings. The **Ball-Game Hall** ❿ (Míčovna), built in 1569 with a sgraffito facade, has a modern greenhouse signed Eva Jiřičná, while at the end of the gardens is the **Belvedere** ⓫ (Belvedér), built in 1537 as a summer palace.

Food and Drink

❶ **LVÍ DVŮR**
U Prašného mostu 6; tel: 224 372 361; daily 11am–11pm; €€
The food here is mostly Czech although there are a few lighter, Italian-inspired dishes. Its small outdoor café has views over the cathedral and the palace gardens.

Archbishop's Palace

NATIONAL GALLERY TO THE LORETA

Away from the bustle of the castle, Hradčany reveals itself to be one of the most pleasant parts of the city, with charming old lanes to explore, ancient churches and three major sites of the National Gallery collections.

DISTANCE: 1km (0.75 mile)
TIME: A half day
START: Hradčanské náměstí
END: Nový Svět
POINTS TO NOTE: A much quieter route than the one through the castle grounds, but no less interesting.

Beyond the castle, Hradčany stretches up to the top of Petřín Hill. In between are atmospheric backstreets, imposing Renaissance and Baroque palaces – three of which are now important art galleries – as well as Prague's holiest pilgrimage site.

HRADČANY SQUARE

Climb up the steep road of Nerudova from Malostranské náměstí and at the top turn right onto Ke Hradu, a switchback that will bring you out onto **Hradčany Square**

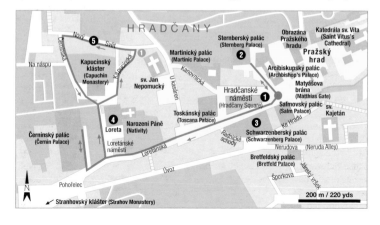

Loreta frescoes   *The finely decorated walls of the Schwarzenberg Palace*

❶ (Hradčanské náměstí). This large open space leads, on one side, into the castle via the Matthias Gate, and in the other direction towards the Loreto Church and Strahov Monastery. In the centre of the square is an ornate Art Nouveau lamppost, somewhat out of place in the Renaissance and Baroque surroundings.

National Gallery

With your back to the castle, on the right-hand side of the square is the **Archbishop's Palace** (Arcibiskupský palác), dating from the 16th century but with a delightful mid-18th-century rococo facade. Pass through the left-hand gateway of the palace and take the passage leading downhill to the **Šternberg Palace** ❷ (Šternberský palác; www.ngprague.cz; Tue–Sun 10am–6pm). This houses the National Gallery's collection of European painting from the Classical era to the end of the Baroque. The collection contains some exceptional works from European Old Masters: *Feast of the Rosary* (1506) by Albrecht Dürer; the two-sided *Hohenburg Altar* (1509) by Hans Holbein the Elder; Rembrandt's *The Scholar in His Study* (1634); and a portrait of *Eleonora of Toledo* (1540–3) by Bronzino.

Schwarzenberg Palace

Opposite the Archbishop's Palace you will see the sgraffito facade of the Renaissance **Schwarzenberg Palace** ❸ (Schwarzenberský palác; www.ngprague.cz; Tue–Sun 10am–6pm). It has been beautifully renovated and is now home to the National Gallery's collection of Baroque art in Bohemia and also includes works from the Late Renaissance. Among the finest works here are *Forest Stream* by Roelant Savery and portraits by Petr Brandl.

Next door, the National Gallery's collection of 19th-century art is displayed in **Salm Palace** (Salmovský palác; www.ngprague.cz; Tue–Sun 10am–6pm), exhibiting important examples of Czech painting and sculpture from Classicism to Romanticism.

LORETA SQUARE

Turn left out of the Schwarzenberg and walk up Loretánská to Loreta Square ❸ (Loretánské náměstí). As you turn right into the square on your left is the long facade of the **Černín Palace (**Černínský palác). The construction of the building, now home to the Czech Foreign Ministry, was so lavish that it made Emperor Leopold I jealous.

The Loreta

Opposite the palace is one of Prague's most important religious complexes, the **Loreta** ❹ (Lorentánské náměsti 7; www.loreta.cz; daily Apr–Oct 9am–5pm, Nov–Mar 9.30am–4pm). The original Loreto is a place of pilgrimage in Italy. In the 13th century, angels are reputed to have brought the Casa Santa, the 'holy house' in which the Archangel Gabriel announced the birth of Jesus to Mary, from the Holy Land to the Italian village of Loreto. Over the years, the

Inside the Loreta

Italian Loreto cult became popular in Bohemia, and Habsburg rulers found this legend well suited to their purpose of returning the heretical Hussites to the true faith. They therefore set about building more than 50 replicas of the 'holy house' across the land; the best-known of these is this one in Prague.

Between 1626 and 1750, a large complex of buildings grew up here, including a chapel, multi-storeyed cloisters, the Church of the Nativity, and an early Baroque tower with a carillon that dates back to 1694. In the courtyard is the Casa Santa (Svatá chyse) itself, built in 1626 by Giovanni Battista Orsi. Most visitors will find the Treasury (see box) the most memorable part of their visit, but don't miss the somewhat over-restored but still amusing frescoes in the cloisters.

NOVÝ SVĚT

Turn right out of the Loreta and take Kapuchinská, the small street that runs to the right from the bottom of the square. At the end of Kapuchinská turn left and you will find yourself in **Nový Svět ⑤**. This line of tiny houses is one of the most attractive streets in Hradčany. While now quite desirable, it was once run-down and mired in poverty – though several famous people have lived here over the centuries, including the astronomer Tycho Brahe, who lived at No. 1, the 'Golden Horn' (U zlatého rohu). If you are in need of refreshment, **U Zlaté Hrušky**, see ①, at No. 3 is a good place to stop.

The Treasure Chamber

The Loreta's main attraction is the Treasure Chamber. As in other places of pilgrimage, pilgrims over the years have given votive gifts to the treasury as a sign of thanksgiving. The gifts of the Bohemian nobility were commissioned from notable goldsmiths of the time and include some of the most valuable works of liturgical art in Central Europe. The most remarkable is the diamond monstrance, which was a legacy of Ludmilla Eva Franziska of Kolowrat. The monstrance, made in 1699 by Baptist Kanischbauer and Matthias Stegner of Vienna to a design by Johann Bernard Fischer von Erlach, is studded with 6,222 diamonds and sends out its rays like the sun. It measures almost 1 metre (3ft) in height and weighs more than 12kg (26lbs).

Food and Drink

① U ZLATÉ HRUŠKY

Nový Svět 3; tel: 220 941 244; www.restaurantuzlatehrusky.cz; daily 11am–1am; €€€
The 'Golden Pear' is an attractive restaurant with a garden section on one of Hradčany's loveliest streets. The menu is a good mix of international and Czech dishes, including roast duck, lamb knuckles and, fittingly, an amazing pear tart.

The view from Petřín Hill.

STRAHOV MONASTERY AND PETŘÍN HILL

From the confines of the Strahov Monastery, stroll out onto the verdant slopes of Petřín Hill and enjoy panoramic views of the city from the observation tower, or else views of the sky from the observatory.

DISTANCE: 2km (1.25 miles)
TIME: 2–3 hours
START: Pohořelec
END: Újezd
POINTS TO NOTE: Tram No 22 stops at Pohořelec. Further along its route, tram No. 22 also stops near the bottom of the funicular railway on Újezd.

The route begins at Pohořelec, the square at the southwestern corner of Hradčany (the Castle District). On the south side of the square, go through the passage between the shops at No. 8 to enter the precinct of the Strahov Monastery. Alternative access is via the path that leads off Úvoz just nearby – where, if you start your walk around midday, you can also have lunch at **Malý Buddha** before you begin, see ❶.

STRAHOV MONASTERY

The **Strahov Monastery** ❶ (Strahovský klášter, Strahovské nádvoří 1; www.strahovskyklaster.cz) was established by King Vladislav II in 1140 for the Premonstratensian Order. It is the oldest monastery in Bohemia and has had an eventful history. It was burnt down in 1258, damaged in the Hussite and Thirty Years' wars and by a French bombardment in 1742, and was occupied by the Prussian army in the decades that followed. In 1952, all religious orders in Czechoslovakia were dissolved by the Communist authorities and it became a museum of literature. In 1990, though, the monks reclaimed their home and can be seen once again in thoughtful perambulation around the fruit trees of Petřín Hill.

Monastery Church

At the centre of the complex is the Church of the Annunciation of Our Lady (Nanebevzetí Panny Marie), which, although substantially remodelled by Anselmo Lurago in 1750, retains elements of the original Romanesque basilica built in 1143. Much of the decorative work you see today was executed by the Czech artist Jiří Neunhertz and depicts scenes from the life of St Norbert, Archbishop of Magdeburg and

founder of the Premonstratensian Order in northern France in 1120. His remains were brought here in 1627 and interred in the chapel of St Ursula to the left of the nave. The church's organ was played by Mozart on at least two occasions.

Library

The monastery's main attraction for visitors today, though, is the **Library** – one of the most beautiful and extensive in the country (daily 9am–noon, 1–5pm). The collection was established at the time of the foundation over 800 years ago, and comprises some 200,000 volumes in the two halls on view to the public and in the adjacent storage facilities. On the facade of the library building is a medallion featuring the portrait of Emperor Joseph II, who, in support of the Enlightenment, dissolved the majority of Bohemia's monasteries in 1783, but spared the Strahov. The Premonstratensians escaped dissolution by presenting their foundation as being primarily educational, and took advantage of the misfortune of other monasteries by acquiring many valuable collections. Further additions from the libraries of defunct monasteries came after World War II.

Inside, the first of the two library halls is the **Philosophers' Hall** (Filozofický sál), built by Ignaz Palliardi in 1782–4. The gilded walnut fittings came from the Bruck Monastery near Znojmo, which had just been dissolved. The rococo ceiling fresco is the work of Franz Anton

The monastery's magnificent library

Maulbertsch and was completed in only six months. It shows the development of humanity through wisdom, in tune with the prevailing Enlightenment ethos. At the two narrow ends you can see Moses with the tablets of law, and opposite, St Paul preaches at the pagan altar. The figure of Divine Providence is enthroned in the centre. On the longer sides of the hall are the great figures of history, from Adam and Eve to the Greek philosophers who made progress possible through their words and deeds.

The second hall is the **Theologians' Hall** (Teologický sál), built by Giovanni Domenico Orsi in 1671–9 in a rich Baroque style. The frescoes were painted by Siardus Nosecký, a member of the Order, between 1723 and 1727. The theme is true wisdom, rooted in the knowledge of God. One of the cabinets lining the walls is barred: it contains books once banned by Church censors. In the middle of the room stand a number of valuable astronomical globes from the Netherlands, dating from the 17th century.

On display just outside the hall is a facsimile of one of the library's prize possessions, the 10th-century Strahov Gospel Book. In a bookcase nearby is the *Xyloteka* (1825), a set of books describing different tree species. Each book is bound in the wood and bark of a different tree, with samples of leaves, roots, flowers and fruits inside.

In the passage between the two libraries are cabinets of curiosities, mostly sea creatures from the collection of Karel Jan Erben, acquired by the monastery in 1798. Among the exhibits is a faked chimera and two whales' penises (next to the model ship and narwhal tusk). There is also a case containing a miniature coffee service made for the Habsburg empress Marie Louise in 1813, which fits into four false books.

Art Museum

The **Strahov Picture Gallery** (daily 9.30–11.30am, noon–5pm) can be found in the second courtyard, accessed behind the monastery church. The works of art are mostly religious, though there are also secular works by Baroque and rococo painters, including Norbert Grund (1717–67) and Franz Anton Maulbertsch (1724–96). One of the most important works on display is the wooden *Strahov Madonna*, by a mid-14th-century Czech sculptor. There is also a wonderful *Judith* from the workshop of Lucas Cranach the Elder (1472–1553).

Miniature Museum

A final attraction within the monastery precinct is the **Miniature Museum** (Strahovské nádvoří 11; www.muzeum miniatur.cz; daily 9am–5pm). Here you can observe the handiwork of Siberian technician Anatoly Konyenko, with the aid of microscopes arranged around the walls of two small rooms. Mr Konyenko used to manufacture tools for eye microsurgery, but has since diverted his talents to inscribing a prayer on a

The Mirror Maze

human hair, creating images of cars on the leg of a mosquito, fitting camels into the eye of a needle, fashioning a pair of horseshoes for a flea and making the world's smallest book.

PETŘÍN HILL

Leaving the monastery by the east gate, you emerge onto Petřín Hill (Petřínské sady). The park was formed by linking up the gardens that had gradually replaced vineyards and a quarry (which provided the stone for the city's buildings). Turn right along the path, with the fruit trees on the slopes to your left, and when you come to some flights of steps, turn right for the final ascent to the top of the hill.

Controversial memorial

At the base of Petřín Hill, near the funicular railway station and opposite the Újezd tram stop, is the stepped *Memorial to the victims of Communism (Pomník obětem komunismu)* with bronze figures in progressive states of decay, created by Czech sculptor Olbram Zoubek in 2002. A bronze strip runs along the centre of the memorial detailing the numbers of those who died in prison, were shot trying to escape or were executed. Unfortunately, the memorial has not been well received; many people object that there are no female figures, and one of the statues was destroyed during a bomb attack in 2003.

Observation Tower

At the top, there is a café (and toilets), where you can recuperate. Then, when you are ready, there are 299 more steps to climb, this time up the **Observation Tower ❷** (Rozhledna; tel: 257 320 112; daily Apr–Sept 10am–10pm, Mar and Oct 10am–8pm, Nov–Feb 10am–6pm). At 60 metres (197ft), this replica of the Eiffel Tower is only a fifth of the height of the original, but offers spectacular views of the city (and in good weather, even to the forests of Central Bohemia). It was constructed out of old railway tracks in 31 days for Prague's 1891 Jubilee Exhibition. During the Nazi occupation, however, Hitler wanted to have it removed because he felt it ruined the view from his room in the castle.

The Maze

Just beyond the tower, and also built for the 1891 Exhibition, is the **Mirror Maze ❸** (Zrcadlové bludiště; tel: 257 315 212; opening times as for the tower). Popular with children, this cast-iron mock-Gothic castle has its own drawbridge and turrets. Inside is a hall of distorting mirrors as well as a wax diorama of the battle between the Praguers and the Swedes in 1648 on the Charles Bridge. Outside again, just opposite is the Church of St Lawrence (kostel sv. Vavřince), a Romanesque building with a Baroque facade.

The Observatory

Retracing your steps towards the tower, turn left through the opening in the mas-

Springtime on Petřín Hill

Petřín Hill Observation Tower

sive wall. This is the so-called **Hunger Wall** (Hladová zed'), which was commissioned by Charles IV in 1362 as a form of 'New Deal' strategy to provide work for the impoverished.

At this point, take the path to the left to reach the **Observatory** ❹ (Štefánikova hvězdárna; www.observatory.cz; opening times vary, but generally Tue–Fri 2–7pm, Sat–Sun 11am–7pm, also 9–11pm during summer). During the day, the 1928 Zeiss telescope is trained on Mercury and Venus as well as sunspots; on clear nights it looks out at the moon, stars and planets.

FUNICULAR RAILWAY

To finish the route, retrace your steps back along the Hunger Wall to the station for the **Funicular Railway** ❺ (lanová dráha; www.dpp.cz; daily 9am–11.30pm; every 10 minutes in summer, 15 minutes in winter; normal tram and metro tickets are valid). When first built in 1891, the train going up the hill was powered solely by the weight of the other one coming down – the cars had water tanks, which were filled at the top and emptied at the bottom. From the 1960s, however, the railway underwent reconstruction and finally reopened in 1985, powered by more modern means. There is no wheelchair access.

If, on reaching the bottom of the hill, you have worked up an appetite, turn right (south) on **Újezd** and left into Vítzná for the **Savoy Café** and **Kolkovna Olympia**, see ❷ and ❸.

Food and Drink

❶ MALÝ BUDDHA

Úvoz 46; tel: 220 513 894; www.maly buddha.cz; Tue–Sun noon–10.30pm; €€

Bizarre and incongruous it may be, but this is one of the better-value restaurants in tourist-thronged Hradčany, and a relaxing haven. This candlelit oriental teahouse serves good, mostly vegetarian food (spring rolls, noodles, Thai curries), as well as numerous varieties of tea, and ginseng wine.

❷ SAVOY CAFÉ

Vítězná 5; tel: 257 311 562; www.cafes avoy.ambi.cz; Mon–Fri 8am–10.30pm, Sat–Sun 9am–10.30pm; €€

Smart café-restaurant that is good for breakfast, lunch, dinner or for just coffee and cake. The menu includes fried eggs with black truffles, roast pike, and curd cheese dumplings stuffed with fruit.

❸ KOLKOVNA OLYMPIA

Vítězná 7; tel: 251 511 080; www. kolkovna.cz; daily 11am–midnight; €€

A restaurant has operated out of this building almost since it was built in 1903. The present incarnation is as a smart bar-restaurant licensed from the Pilsner Urquell Brewery. The emphasis is on comforting Czech butchery, goose, duck, sausages, boar rump, pork hock, lamb knuckle, though it also extends to risotto, pasta and salads. The cooking is highly creditable, as is the value for money.

CHARLES BRIDGE AND MALÁ STRANA

Occupying the slopes between the river and the castle, Malá Strana, or 'Lesser Town', is the most intact Baroque townscape in Central Europe. Its winding cobbled streets and attractive burghers' houses seem straight out of a fairy tale.

DISTANCE: 4km (2.5 miles)
TIME: A full day
START: Charles Bridge
END: Kampa Park
POINTS TO NOTE: Start early in the morning to beat the crowds and see the bridge in the mist.

Malá Strana (Lesser Town) lies at the foot of Prague Castle, separated from the rest of the city by parks and the River Vltava. From humble beginnings in the 9th century, it was elevated to the status of a town in 1257 (the second-oldest of the five towns that originally formed Prague) by the Přemyslid ruler, Otakar II. Merchants were then invited from Germany to set up shop on the land beneath the castle walls.

The town experienced its first boom during the reign of Charles IV (1346–78), when it was extended and received new fortifications. It subsequently suffered major damage in 1419 during the Hussite Wars, and in the Great Fire of 1541, when catastrophic damage necessitated a major rebuilding programme.

Malá Strana truly blossomed after the victory of the Catholic League over the Bohemians in the Battle of White Mountain in 1620, which concluded the Bohemian phase of the Thirty Years' War. In the redistribution of property that followed, many wealthy families loyal to the House of Habsburg settled here on the parcels of land they had received. The court later moved back to Vienna and most of the palaces were deserted. They were, however, kept intact and have been spared major alteration to this day. Even the town houses, which often have much older foundations, have retained their Baroque facades and characteristic house signs.

CHARLES BRIDGE

Start at **Charles Bridge ❶** (Karlův most), commissioned by Charles IV in 1357 to replace the earlier Judith Bridge, which collapsed in a flood in 1342. Completed *c.*1400, it was built by Petr Parléř (who also designed St Vitus's Cathedral) and has withstood centuries of traffic and numerous floods, thanks, so legend has it, to the use of eggs in the mortar.

The ever-popular Charles Bridge

Staré Město side of the bridge

On the Staré Město side of the bridge is Parléř's **Old Town Bridge Tower** (Staroměstská mostecká věž; http://en.muzeumprahy.cz/prague-towers; daily Apr–Sept 10am–10pm, Mar and Oct until 8pm, Nov–Feb until 6pm). It was here that in 1648, at the end of the Thirty Years' War, an army of Swedish invaders was fought off by a band of Prague locals. Despite some damage, much of the sculptural decoration survives. Look on the external corners for the figures of 14th-century gropers feeling up buxom ladies.

Inside the tower is an exhibition but the real draw is the 138-step climb to the viewing gallery on the roof.

Crossing the bridge, you pass a series of statues and monuments, the majority of which are copies of the Baroque originals. The earliest of these is a crucifix (third on the right) erected in 1657. In 1696, a Jewish man was found guilty of blaspheming in front of the crucifix and was made to pay for the gold Hebrew inscription that reads, 'Holy, Holy, Holy Lord God Almighty'.

The most famous statue on the bridge is that of **St John of Nepomuk** (eighth on the right), placed here in 1683. King Wenceslas IV was supposed to have had this priest killed after he refused to divulge the contents of the queen's confession; he was dressed up in a suit of armour and thrown over the side of the bridge.

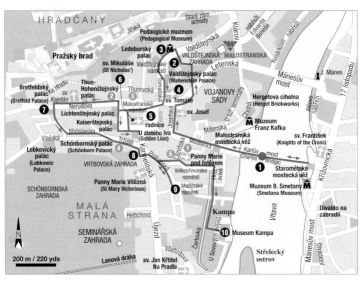

St John of Nepomuk being thrown off the bridge

Other important statues include that of **St Luitgard** (fourth from end on the left), sculpted by Matthias Braun in 1710 and often considered the finest work on the bridge, and the **group featuring SS John of Matha and Félix de Valois**. In the 12th century, these two saints founded the Trinitarian Order to raise ransoms for crusaders captured by the Turks. Inexplicably, St Ivan has also gatecrashed the group.

Before entering Malá Strana, you first encounter two towers. The shorter one was originally part of the 12th-century **Judith Bridge** that preceded the Charles Bridge. The taller one (on the right) is the **Malá Strana Bridge Tower** (Malostranská mostecká věž; http://en.muzeum prahy.cz/prague-towers; daily Apr–Sept 10am–10pm, Mar and Oct until 8pm, Nov–Feb until 6pm) and was built from 1464 in imitation of the tower at the Staré Město end of the bridge. Inside is an exhibition on the history of the bridge, though it is the views from the top that justify the entrance fee.

NORTHERN MALÁ STRANA

Mostecká
Passing under the bridge tower, you emerge onto **Mostecká** (Bridge Street). If you want a snack before continuing the walk, make a detour to **Bohemia Bagel**, see ❶, off to the left on Lázenská.

Back on Mostecká, among the fine Baroque houses is the 18th-century Kaunitz Palace at No. 15, now the Serbian Embassy. Further up, turn right onto Josefská. At the end of the street on your right is the pretty Baroque Church of St Joseph, which was restored to the Loreto Sisters (founded by Mary Ward in 1609) in 1989.

Waldstein Palace and Gardens
Turning right onto Letenská, walk on until you find a doorway in the high wall on your left. This is the entrance to the gardens of the **Waldstein (or Wallenstein) Palace** ❷ (Valdštejnský palác; www.senat.cz; gardens Apr–Oct daily 7.30am–6pm, palace Apr–Oct Sat–Sun 10am–5pm; free). This was the first Baroque palace in Prague, built from 1624–30 by Italian architects for the opportunistic General Albrecht von Wallenstein (1583–1634). Take a stroll around the beautiful gardens before heading to the palace on the far side.

The gardens are overlooked by a triple-arched loggia (*sala terrena*), decorated with frescoes of scenes from the Trojan War. It was here that Wallenstein dined during the 12 months he lived in the palace. On the western side of the gardens is a large aviary (home to several owls) and an extraordinary artificial grotto with stalactites and grotesques. Elsewhere around the garden are bronze statues of mythological figures – the work of Adriaen de Vries, court sculptor to Emperor Rudolf II. Unfortunately, these are only copies; the originals were taken to Sweden as spoils of war in 1648 and are now in the park of Drottningholm Palace near Stockholm. At the gardens'

Busy Malá Strana   *Waldstein Palace*

eastern end are a large ornamental pond and a former Riding School, where temporary exhibitions are now held.

The palace itself matches Wallenstein's grand political ambitions – by 1625 he owned a quarter of all Bohemia – and was intended to rival Prague Castle. Today it houses the Czech Senate, although various rooms are open to the public.

The main hall has ceiling paintings by Baccio di Bianca, which feature Wallenstein depicted as Mars, god of war, riding his chariot to battle. Next is the Knights' Hall, with its unusual 19th-century leather wall covering, and then the circular Audience Chamber and the Mythological Corridor, decorated with scenes from Ovid and Virgil.

Pedagogical Museum

Exit the palace onto Valdštejnská and turn left to reach Waldstein Square. On your right is the **Pedagogical Museum ❸** (Tue–Sat 10am–12.30pm and 1–5pm), charting the development of education based on the works of the Czech philosopher Comenius (1592–1670). Off the square to your left is Tomáška.

Tomáška

Walking along Tomáška you pass several fine Baroque houses, including **The Golden Stag** and **The Golden Pretzel** (No. 12). These house signs date from the time before house numbers were introduced (in 1770 by Joseph II). They were based on the profession or craft of the house owner, his status, or the immediate environment of the house. Animals and other symbolic signs, of both a secular and a religious nature, were popular. If ownership of the house changed, the house retained its original sign – and sometimes the new owner even took the name of the house himself.

St Thomas's Church

At the end of the street on the left is **St Thomas's Church ❹** (Kostel sv. Tomáše; Josefská 8; www.augustiniani.cz; Mon–Sat 11am–1pm, Sun 9am–noon, 4.30–5.30pm; free). The church is the most impressive part of a former Augustinian monastery founded in the 13th century. Its present Baroque form (late 1720s) is the work of Kilián Ignaz Dientzenhofer. The church originally had two altarpieces by Rubens (the Martyrdom of St Thomas and St Augustine), now replaced by copies (the originals are in the National Gallery's Šternberg Palace; see page 33). The ceiling frescoes are by the Bohemian artist Václav Vavřinec Reiner. Next door are cloisters and what was once the monastic brewery (founded in 1358).

Lesser Town Square

At the end of Tomáška is the **Lesser Town Square ❺** (Malostranské náměstí). On the lower side of the square at No. 21 is the quarter's old town hall, while at No. 18 is the Smiřický Palace, where Protestant nobles planned the second Prague defenestration in 1618 (see box). On the other (west) side of the square is

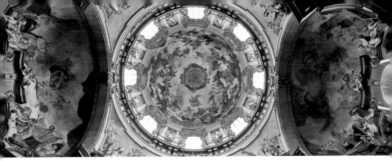

The dome of St Nicholas's Church

the **Lichtenstein Palace**, with its broad classical facade. From 1620 to 1627 it belonged to Karl von Lichtenstein, the so-called 'Bloody Governor', who was chiefly responsible for the execution of the leaders of the 1618 rebellion.

Nearby, the **Kaiserstein Palace** bears a plaque memorialising the opera singer Ema Destinová, who once lived there. On the south side of the square at No. 10 is the **Golden Lion House**, one of the few purely Renaissance houses remaining in the Malá Strana.

St Nicholas's Church

Dominating the square is the **Church of St Nicholas ❻** (Kostel sv. Mikuláše; www.stnicholas.cz; Mar–Oct 9am–5pm, Nov–Feb 9am–4pm), probably Prague's finest Baroque building and a potent symbol of the Counter-Reformation. It was started in the early 18th century by the Bavarian architect Christoph Dientzenhofer, who designed the facade, nave and side chapels. His son, Kilián Ignaz, added the choir and the dome, and then Anselmo Lurago completed the building with a tower in 1755. Except in winter, it is possible to ascend the tower for fine views.

The church's newly restored interior features one of the largest ceiling frescoes in Europe in the nave. Painted by Johann Lukas Kracker in 1770, it portrays scenes from the life of St Nicholas. Meanwhile, the 75-metre (247ft) high dome is decorated with František Xaver Palko's *Celebration of the Holy Trinity*.

You can get an excellent view of the frescoes from the gallery above the nave (the entrance via the steps lies to the left of the main altar). The gallery also displays Karel Škréta's *Passion* cycle (1673–4).

In front of the four pillars supporting the dome is a set of sculptures of the Eastern Church Fathers (executed 1755–69) by Ignác František Platzer. He was also responsible for the gilded statue of *St Nicholas* (1765) by the high altar, designed by Andrey Pozza. The ornate pulpit is made of artificial marble and covered with gilt (from the workshop of R.J. Prachner, 1762–6). The church's 2,500-pipe organ, completed in 1746 before the building itself was finished, is supposed to have been

Defenestration

Czech history is strewn with defenestrations (the act of throwing someone out of a window). The tradition began in 1419 when the Hussites threw seven Catholic town councillors from the New Town Hall. It continued in 1618 when two imperial councillors and their secretary were thrown from Prague Castle. In 1948, Jan Masaryk, the Foreign Minister was found dead in the courtyard of the Foreign Ministry, below his bathroom window. Three separate investigations by Communist authorities all came to the conclusion of death by suicide. A 2004 police investigation, however, concluded that he had been defenestrated by political foes.

Trams on Malostranské náměstí

played by Mozart in 1787. On his death in 1791, his famous *Requiem* was performed in the church as a tribute.

Outside again, the massive block next door is a former Jesuit College, while in the middle of the square is a plague column by Giovanni Alliprandi (1715). To continue the route, now make for the northwest corner of the square and Nerudova.

Nerudova

Nerudova street is named after the Czech poet and author Jan Neruda (1834–91), who lived at No. 47, U dvou slunc ů (The Two Suns). His work, particularly *Tales of the Lesser Quarter*, was inspired by the everyday life of Malá Strana.

Before you walk up the street you could stop off for refreshments at **U Kocoura** at No. 2 on your right, or else at **U Hrocha** on the street behind it, see ❷ and ❸.

Many of the middle-class houses on Nerudova were originally built in a Renaissance style and later given Baroque facades. Most have house signs: **The Three Violins** (several generations of violin-makers lived here) at No. 12, **The Golden Chalice** at No. 16, **St John of Nepomuk** at No. 18 and **The Donkey and the Cradle** at No. 25. A pharmacy was formerly housed in **The Golden Lion** at No. 32.

Two embassies have settled into the Baroque palaces in this street. On the left at No. 5 is the **Morzin Palace** (1714), now the Romanian Embassy. Its facade is ornamented with the work of Ferdinand Maximilian Brokoff: Moors supporting the balcony, allegorical figures of Day and Night, and sculptures representing the four corners of the world. Further up at No. 20 is the Thun-Hohenstein Palace (1726), which is now the Italian Embassy, decorated (by Matthias Bernard Braun) with two eagles with outspread wings; and statues of Jupiter and Juno.

Next to the palace is the **Church of Our Lady of Perpetual Succour**, which operated as a theatre from 1834 to 1837, presenting numerous plays during the Czech National Revival. On the other side of the road, Neruda's house at No. 47 has long since functioned as a pub. In the Communist era, it was a favourite meeting place for the Plastic People of the Universe, the underground rock band whose arrest prompted Václav Havel and others to found Charter 77, the petition against the governing regime's human rights violations.

SOUTHERN MALÁ STRANA

Below Nerudova

Retracing your steps a little, at No. 33 you find the rococo **Bretfeld Palace** ❼ (Bretfeldský palác) with a relief of St Nicholas on the portal. Lavish balls once took place here, some of which Mozart and Casanova are said to have attended. Close by, the Jánský Vršek steps lead down the hill. Look out for the turning off to the left onto Břetisalova, at the end of which turn right into Tržiště.

Vrtba Gardens, a World Heritage Site

Continue past the 17th-century Schön-born Palace – now the heavily guarded US Embassy – and on to No. 7: **Gitanes**, see ❹, a good place to stop for a hearty meal. At the end of the road, turn right.

Just around the corner on Karmelitská is the gate to the **Vrtba Gardens** ❽ (Vrtbovská zahrada; www.vrtbovska.cz; Apr–Oct daily 10am–6pm). This World Heritage Site offers perhaps the finest example of Baroque landscaping in Prague. The garden hosts sculptures by Matthias Bernhard Braun and a pavilion with frescoes by Václav Vavřinec Reiner. On the other side of Karmelitská is the turning for Prokopská, which leads down to Maltézské náměstí.

Maltese Square

Maltese Square ❾ (Maltézské náměstí) takes its name from the fact that for centuries the Knights of Malta lived in the vicinity. In 1169, they founded a monastery just behind where the Gothic Church of Our Lady Beneath the Chain (Panny Marie pod řetězem) stands today, at the junction with Lázeňská. The 'chain' of the church's name is a reference to the barrier used by the knights to guard the Judith Bridge (the Charles Bridge's prior incarnation). It is the oldest surviving church in Malá Strana, though the remains of its 12th-century Romanesque predecessor can still be seen in the right-hand wall of the forecourt. Opposite the church, on Lázeňská, is a good pitstop, **Cukrkávalimonáda**, see ❺.

Adjacent to the Church of Our Lady Beneath the Chain is another square, **Velkopřevorské náměstí**. On one side is the **Buquoy Palace**, home to the French Embassy, and opposite is the former **Palace of the Grand Prior of the Knights of Malta**, one of the most beautiful in the area. The wall of the Palace of the Grand Prior, facing the French Embassy, is known as the **John Lennon Wall**.

During the 1980s, this graffiti-strewn wall was the focus of Prague's Beatles-worship. The 'mural', with its depiction of John Lennon, was twice under threat; first from the secret police, who painted it over, and then from the Knights of Malta, when it had been repainted and the property returned to them under the post-1989 restitution. The wall was finally saved by the intervention of the French ambassador, who appealed to the authorities to let it be.

Kampa Island

Continuing the route (with the wall on your left), go straight on at the crossroads and over the small river – the Čertovka, or Devil's Stream – onto **Kampa Island**. This little district is sometimes referred to as Little Venice on account of its situation, water mills and gardens. Turn right at the end of the road on to Hroznová then head south.

Much of the southern part of the island is given over to Kampa Park, a green space formed in 1940 by linking up the gardens of former palaces. Bounded by water on both sides, it has remained undeveloped because of the constant risk of flooding.

Continue south through the park along U Lužického Semináře and then take the path off to your left towards the river bank and the **Kampa Museum** ❿ (Museum

John Lennon Wall   *The Čertovka river along Kampa Island*

Kampa; www.museumkampa.com; daily 10am–6pm). The building is a converted water mill with modern additions: a staircase leads up to a glass cube (by Marian Kasměla) on top of the building, and excellent views. There is also a glass footbridge (by Václav Cigler), which appears to lead you out over the river. The proximity of the river ensured that the museum was inundated by the 2002 floods. The large sculp-ture of a chair on the embankment outside was washed 40km (25 miles) downstream.

Based around the collections of wealthy Czech expats Jan and Meda Mladek, the museum holds works by the abstract painter František Kupka (1871–1963) and the Expressionist and Cubist sculptor Otto Gutfreund (1889–1927). A substantial portion of the space is given over to contemporary Central European art.

Food and Drink

① BOHEMIA BAGEL

Lázeňská 19; tel: 257 218 192; www.bohemiabagel.cz; daily 7.30am–6pm, Sat–Sun until 7pm; €

American-style café, serving fresh bagels and sandwiches, cooked breakfasts (until 2pm), pancakes, muffins, salads, quiches and burgers. Free refills of coffee and soft drinks. Wine and beer also on offer. Wi-Fi available.

② U KOCOURA

Nerudova 2; tel: 257 530 107; daily noon–11pm; €

The Tomcat pub used to be owned by the Friends of Beer, which was once a political party, but now merely a civic association. Despite the location, prices are reasonable.

③ U HROCHA

Thunovské 10; tel: 257 533 389; daily noon–11.30pm; €

The Hippo is one of the few places in the district still aimed at local residents. Simple wooden furniture, a smoky atmosphere, excellent beer and basic high-carb food to soak up the alcohol.

④ GITANES

Tržiště 7; tel: 257 530 163; www.gitanes.cz; daily noon–midnight; €€€

Cosy restaurant specialising in the cuisine of the former Yugoslavia, complete with flowery tablecloths, and Naïve paintings and farm implements on the walls. On the menu: sauerkraut filled with mince and rice, lamb sausages and boiled apples filled with nuts and topped with whipped cream.

⑤ CUKRKÁVALIMONÁDA

Lázeňská 7; tel: 257 225 396; www.cukrkava limonada.com; daily 9am–7pm; €€

Ideal for a drink, lunch or afternoon tea away from the crowds, 'Sugar-coffee-lemonade' is a beautiful café offering scrambled eggs and bacon for breakfast, pastas, frittatas, pancakes, soup and sandwiches all day. Also home-made pastries and cakes and speciality hot chocolate.

Close-up of the Astronomical Clock

STARÉ MĚSTO

Staré Město, or the Old Town, has more to offer than Baroque churches and cobbled streets. This route takes in an astronomical clock, a jewel thief's mummified arm, Mozart's theatre and an eccentric collection of tribal art.

DISTANCE: 3km (2 miles)
TIME: A full day
START: Charles Bridge
END: Ethnographic Museum
POINTS TO NOTE: You may decide to do this walk in two instalments: first Western Staré Město and the Old Town Square, then Southern Staré Město.

Staré Město, or the Old Town, is situated on the right bank of the Vltava. The pattern of its streets and squares has remained largely unaltered since the Middle Ages. Its perimeter is marked by streets that trace the lines of the former city walls – Národní třída, Na příkopě and Revoluční.

Originally the Old Town lay some 2–3 metres (6–9ft) below the modern street level but the area proved vulnerable to flooding, and consequently the street level has been raised little by little since the late 13th century. Many of the district's houses still have Romanesque rooms hidden in their basements.

WESTERN STARÉ MĚSTO

The walk begins by the Charles Bridge in Křižovnické náměstí (Knights of the Cross Square). The Knights of the Cross were founded as a crusader order of monks in the early 13th century and established themselves here not long afterwards. Since 1989, they have reclaimed their property on the northern side of the square.

Here can be found their domed Baroque Church of St Francis, built by the French architect Jean-Baptiste Mathey from 1679 to 1685. Its ornate interior features frescoes by Václav Vavřinec Reiner and Jan Krystof Lisk. Next door, in the order's former hospital, is the **Charles Bridge Museum** (www.prague-bridge.com; daily 10am–6pm). As well as an exhibition on the history of the bridge, you can see the foundations of the Judith Bridge, which was swept away by floods in 1342. There is also access here to an underground chapel decorated in grotto style, with stalactites made out of dust and eggshells.

Old Town rooftops

Smetana Museum

On a small spit of land just to the south of the Charles Bridge is the **Smetana Museum** (Muzeum Bedřicha Smetany; www.nm.cz; Wed–Mon 10am–5pm), dedicated to the nationalist composer Bedřich Smetana (1824–84). Housed in a neo-Renaissance former municipal waterworks, the museum illustrates the life and work of the father of Czech music.

Clementinum

Back at the bridge, across the road is the Baroque facade of St Salvator, part of the sprawling complex of the **Clementinum ❶** (Klementinum; www.klementinum.com; grounds daily 6am–11pm, free; access to the Baroque Library Hall and Astronomical Tower by guided tour only, daily

every 30 minutes from 10am–4.30pm). This college was founded in 1556 by the Jesuits, who had been summoned to the country by the Habsburgs to spearhead the Counter-Reformation and cancel out the revolutionary ideas promulgated by the Protestant Karolinum University (of which Jan Hus had once been rector). As the Jesuits' wealth accrued, they bought up churches, gardens and 30 houses to extend their precinct.

In 1773, however, not long after the buildings were finally completed, Joseph II forced the Jesuits into exile in enthusiastic compliance with the Pope's decree to suppress the order. Today, the Clementinum is part of Charles University.

Enter by the gate just to the left of St Salvator. Cross the first courtyard and walk

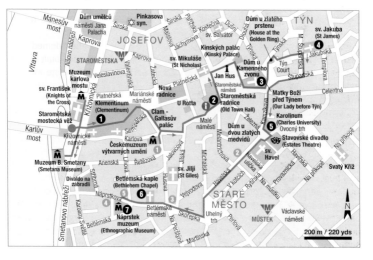

through the arch. Immediately on your left is the **National Library** (www.nkp.cz), with a collection of 6 million volumes. On your right is the **Church of St Clement,** which is often open to visitors. Its exuberant Baroque interior was designed by Kilián Dientzenhofer in 1715. It now ministers to a Greek Orthodox congregation. Just behind it is the oval-shaped Italian Chapel, which can be seen from the street outside, but is closed to the public. Built around 1590 for the Italian craftsmen working in the complex, it is still technically owned by the Italian government.

At the far end of this second courtyard is the Astronomical Tower on your left. Entrance to the **Baroque Library Hall** is beneath it. Completed in 1722 it houses theological books. The allegorical ceiling frescoes by Jan Hiebl depict antique learning as the basis for Christian teachings.

Above the library is the **Astronomical Tower**, also built in the 1720s and used for observation of the skies until the 1930s. Halfway up you can see the Prague meridian; when sunlight crossed the line at noon, a flag used to be hung from the tower and a cannon fired.

In the next courtyard, through the arch on the left, the **Chapel of Mirrors** is a frequent venue for concerts, during which you can gaze at Jan Hiebl's frescoed ceiling, with strips that illustrate verses of the Hail Mary prayer, and Václav Vavřinec Reiner's murals of scenes from the life of the Virgin Mary. To exit the complex, walk through the gate to the far right-hand corner of the courtyard into Marianské náměstí.

Husova

On the south side of Marianské náměstí on the corner of Husova is the **Clam-Gallas Palace**. This magnificent Baroque building was constructed in 1730 by the Viennese court architect, Johann Bernhard Fischer von Erlach. The portal is ornamented with statues of Hercules by Matthias Bernhard Braun. Once containing a theatre, where Beethoven reputedly performed, the building now houses the city archives.

Heading south along Husova you soon come to a crossroads. Just before turning left (east) onto Karlova, continue a little further on Husova to Nos 19–21; here, behind a Venetian-Renaissance facade, is the **Czech Museum of Fine Arts** (České muzeum výtvarných umění; www.cmvu.cz; Tue–Sun 10am–6pm), which puts on exhibitions of contemporary Bohemian art.

After visiting the museum, you may wish to slake your thirst next door at **U Zlatého tygra** (The Golden Tiger), see ❶, before turning back to Karlova.

Karlova

The narrow and twisting Karlova (Charles Lane) has long been the main link between the Charles Bridge and the Old Town Square and is part of the Royal Way, the processional route followed by Czech kings on their way to St Vitus Cathedral on coronation day. Follow its course east to reach Little Square (Malé náměstí) and the Old Town Square (Staroměstské náměstí).

The Old Town Square in all its glory

OLD TOWN SQUARE

Old Town Hall

Entering Little Square, on your left is the **Old Town Hall** ❷ (Staroměstská radnice; www.staromestkaradnicepraha.cz; tours Mon 11am–10pm, Tue-Sun 9am–6pm). Originally founded in 1338, the complex was composed of a set of medieval buildings, purchased one by one over the years with the proceeds of the city's tax on wine.

The first feature to strike you as you approach is the **Astronomical Clock** (Orloj), which dates from 1410 – although it was transformed into the contraption you see today by one Master Hanuš in 1490. According to legend he was blinded after completing his work, so that he could not replicate it anywhere else. He got his revenge by climbing into the mechanism and disabling it. Documentary evidence suggests, however, that he continued to maintain the clock, unblinded, for many years, though it did not work properly until it was overhauled in 1570.

The performance of the upper part of the clock draws many tourists at the striking every hour on the hour 9am–11pm. Death rings the death knell and turns an hourglass upside down. The 12 Apostles proceed along the little windows that open before the chimes, and a cockerel flaps its wings and crows. The hour strikes. To the right of Death, a Turk wags his head. The two figures on the left are allegories of Greed and Vanity.

The face of the clock underneath preserves the medieval view of the course of the sun and moon through the zodiac, with Prague and the earth located at the centre of the universe. Beneath that is the calendar, with signs of the zodiac and scenes from country life, symbolising the 12 months of the year. The calendar is a replica of the work executed by Czech painter Josef Mánes in 1866 and now in the Prague City Museum.

Tours of the Old Town Hall take in the 15th-century council chamber, Petr Parléř's Gothic chapel (with a view of the interior workings of the clock), as well as the dungeons, which were used by the Czech resistance as its headquarters during the Prague uprising at the end of World War II. Separate tickets can be purchased for access to the stairs or lift up the **tower** (Mon 11am–10pm, Tue–Sun 9am–8pm).

Hus Memorial

Elsewhere in the square, the imposing memorial in the middle honours the great Protestant reformer Jan Hus and was erected on the 500th anniversary – 6 July 1915 – of his being burnt at the stake. The work of Czech sculptor Ladislav Šaloun, it features Hussites and Protestants around the figure of Hus, together with a mother and child symbolising rebirth. Since its unveiling it has formed a symbol of resistance to foreign occupation, from the fall of the Habsburg empire to the invasion of the Warsaw Pact troops in 1968.

St Nicholas's Church

In the northwest corner of the square is the white Baroque **Church of St Nicho-**

Jan Hus Memorial

las (Kostel sv. Mikuláše; daily Mar–Oct 9am–5pm, Nov–Feb 9am–4pm; free), built to designs by Kilián Ignaz Dientzenhofer in 1735. The church owes its unusual proportions to the fact that it was originally hemmed in by houses that stood in front, completely separating it from the square. The dark statues on the outside are by Antonín Braun, a nephew of Matthias Bernhard Braun. The sparse interior is somewhat disappointing, having suffered at the hands of Emperor Joseph II, who closed the monastery connected to the church and used it as a warehouse.

Kinský Palace

In the northeast corner of the square is the rococo **Kinský Palace** (Palác Kinských), also designed by Kilián Ignaz Dientzenhofer. It was from here in February 1948 that Communist leader Klement Gottwald made the speech that heralded in the totalitarian regime. The building now houses the National Gallery's permanent exhibition of the **Art of Asia and the Ancient Mediterranean** (www.ngprague.cz; daily 10am–6pm). The ground-floor bookshop once formed the premises of Franz Kafka's father's haberdashery shop. Young Franz himself attended school elsewhere in the building.

House at the Stone Bell

To the right of the palace, at No. 13, is the 14th-century Gothic **House at the Stone Bell** (Dům u kamenného zvonu; www.ghmp.cz; Tue–Sun 10am–8pm), which hosts temporary exhibitions put on by the Prague City Gallery. The two neighbouring houses are connected by an arcaded passage with ribbed vaulting. The house to the left is the former **Týn School**, originally a Gothic building, but rebuilt in the style of a Venetian Renaissance loggia. On the right is the early neoclassical **House at the White Unicorn** (Dům u bílého jednorožce; daily 10am–8pm), which provides another venue for art exhibitions.

Týn Church

Rising up behind is the **Church of Our Lady before Týn ❸** (Kostel Matky Boží před Týnem; Tue–Sat 10am–1pm, 3–5pm, Sun 10.30am–noon; donation). Built in 1365, the Týn Church is famous for its iconic towers. One of them is actually shorter and thinner than the other, which has led to their being nicknamed Adam and Eve. Until 1621 this was the main church of the Hussites. One of their leaders, George of Poděbrady (1458–71) had a gold chalice set into the gable niche between the church's two towers as a symbol of the Hussite faith. When the Jesuits took over after 1620 it was replaced by a statue of the Virgin, the chalice being melted down to make her crown, halo and sceptre.

To find the church's entrance, walk down the passageway through the arch second from the left of the Týn School's four arches. Inside, the Baroque interior was commissioned by the Jesuits. The paintings on the high altar and on the side altars are by Karel Škréta. Other

The Clock and Týn Church   *Church of St James*

remarkable works of art include the Gothic Madonna (north aisle), the Gothic pulpit, and the oldest remaining font in Prague (1414).

To the right of the high altar is the red marble tombstone of the Danish astronomer Tycho Brahe (1546–1601), who worked at the court of Rudolf II. The inscription on the slab translates as 'Better to be than to seem to be'. Note also the window immediately to the right of the south portal; although now blocked off, it once enabled the occupants of the neighbouring house at Celetná 3 to peer into the church. One resident who enjoyed this privilege was Franz Kafka, who lived there from 1896 to 1907.

Týn Court

Now take the lane called Týnská around the back of the church. On your left on the corner is the Renaissance **House at the Golden Ring** (Dům u zlatého prstenu; www.ghmp.cz; Tue–Sun 10am–8pm), a branch of the Prague City Gallery showing 20th-century Czech art. To the right is the entrance to the Týn Court, also known by its German name, Ungelt. Through the arch is a courtyard, the origins of which go back to the 11th century, when it offered protection to visiting foreign merchants. It is now a beautiful setting for some shops and cafés.

Exiting at the far end of Týn Court, you emerge onto Malá Štupartská. Opposite is the **Church of St James** ❹ (Kostel sv. Jakuba; Mon–Sat 9.30am–noon, 2–4pm, Sun 2–4pm; free). Built by the Minorites during the reign of Charles IV, the church was renovated in the Baroque period. Note the reliefs on the main portal and the ceiling frescoes, the painting on the high altar by Václav Vavřinec Reiner and the extravagant tomb of Count Vratislav Mitrovic, the work of Johann Bernhard Fischer von Erlach and Ferdinand Brokoff.

A more gruesome feature is the 400-year-old decomposed arm hanging on the west wall, supposedly amputated from a thief who tried to steal the jewels from the altar, but who was stopped, legend has it, by the Madonna grabbing his offending arm. The almost theatrical quality of the interior provides a fine setting for the frequent organ concerts given on the uniquely toned instrument dating from 1705.

SOUTHERN STARÉ MĚSTO

Carolinum and Estates Theatre

Leaving the church, head south (left) down Malá Štupartská, turn right onto Štupartská, follow the road round to the end, turn left and cross over Celetná to find the narrow passage to Kamzíkova, beside the Choc-Story Museum (www.choco-story-praha.cz; daily 9.30–7pm). At the end of the lane, turn left and on your right is Charles University or **Carolinum** ❺ (Karolinum), centred around the Gothic Rotlev House at Železná 9.

Founded by Charles IV in 1348, the university soon became associated with the Protestant reformers, and Jan Hus

The Estates Theatre

was rector here from 1402. Around the corner, on the south side, you can see the magnificent oriel window, which is part of the Chapel of SS Cosmas and Damian and the only true remnant of the original 14th-century Gothic building. Today, the complex is used for graduation ceremonies and is closed to the public.

Next door is the neoclassical **Estates Theatre** (Stavovské divadlo; www.narodni-divadlo.cz; see page 118), which originally opened in 1783 as the Nostitz Theatre, named after Count Nostitz, who paid for it. In its earlier history, it played largely to upper-class German audiences, hence its current name – the 'Estates' were the German nobility. Famously, this was where Mozart conducted the première of *Don Giovanni* in 1787. It was also the site, in 1834, of the first performance of the Czech national anthem, *Kde domov můj?* ('Where is My Home?'), originally part of the musical *Fidlovačka*.

Bethlehem Square

Now make your way down Havelská, just opposite the Carolinum. On your left is the 13th-century **Church of St Gall** (Kostel sv. Halva) with its onion domes (added in 1722), while on your right, down Melant-richova is **Country Life**, a rare vegetarian-friendly lunch option, see ❷. At the end of Havelská you come out into Uhelný Trh, once the site of the town's coal market. On the far side of the square, continue down Skořepka, then turn right onto Husova. Soon afterwards is a turning on the left for **Bethlehem Square** (Betlémské náměstí).

Bethlehem Chapel

On the north side of the square, on the right, is the **Bethlehem Chapel** ❻ (Betlémská kaple; www.bethlehemchapel.eu; daily 10am–6pm). It was here that Jan Hus delivered his fiery Reformationist sermons (in Czech rather than Latin) from 1402 until shortly before his martyrdom in 1415. A century later, in 1521, Thomas Münzer, the leader of the German peasants' revolt, also preached here.

The building dates from 1391. Its plain interior, which could hold up to 3,000 people, had the pulpit as its focal point rather than the altar. However, once Protestantism was banned in the 17th century, the building was taken over by the Jesuits, who converted it into a wood store. It was then demolished in 1786. Fortunately, it was meticulously reconstructed in its original form in the early 1950s, partly utilising original building materials. The Communist authorities seem to have viewed Hus as being an authentic working-class hero. Three of the original walls remain, and show heavily restored fragments of the scriptures painted on them to help parishioners follow the service.

On the east side of the chapel precinct is the design gallery, shop and restaurant, **Klub Architektů**, see ❶.

Ethnographic Museum

On the west side of Bethlehem Square is an archway leading to another courtyard and to the **Ethnographic Museum** ❼ (Náprstek muzeum; www.nm.cz; Tue–Sun 10am–6pm). The museum is named

Pretty backstreet   *Bethlehem Chapel*

after Vojta Náprstek (1826–94). His fortune derived from brewing, and he chose to spend it on his two passions – ethnography and technology. His gadgets are now in the **National Technical Museum** (Národní technické muzeum; Kostelní 42; www.ntm.cz) in Holešovice, while his Asian, African and American collections are housed here, in the former brewery. He also established here the country's first women's club, whose meeting room has been preserved just as it was, complete with the hole Náprstek drilled through the wall from his office.

Just around the corner from the museum are two good options for drinks, snacks or more substantial meals: **Café Kampus**, see ❹, and **V Zátiší**, see ❺.

Food and Drink

❶ U ZLATÉHO TYGRA
Husova 17; tel: 222 221 111; www.uzlatehotygra.cz; daily 3–11pm; €
Perhaps the most famous hostelry in Prague, the Golden Tiger was where Václac Havel took Bill Clinton in 1994 to show him a real Czech pub. Unfortunately, since then it has put up its prices and gone for the tourist dollar. Even so, it's a great place to enjoy a Pilsner.

❷ COUNTRY LIFE
Melantrichova 15; tel: 224 213 366; Mon–Thu 10.30am–7.30pm, Fri 10.30am–4:30pm, Sun noon–6pm; €
Run by the Seventh-day Adventists, this is a haven for vegetarians. Line up and take what you want from the salad bar and hot dishes (all food is organically grown). At the checkout, your plate is weighed and the cost calculated.

❸ KLUB ARCHITEKTŮ
Betlémské náměstí 5a; tel: 224 248 878; www.klubarchitektu.com; daily 11.30am–midnight; €€

This place has a bookshop on the ground floor, a first-floor gallery and a restaurant in the cellars. The food is generally Mediterranean in style and always good value for money.

❹ CAFÉ KAMPUS
Náprstkova 10; tel: 775 755 143; www.cafekampus.cz; Mon–Fri 10am–1am, Sat noon–1am (Sun until 11pm); €
Stylish and informal café/wine-bar/gallery also hosting literary evenings and concerts. Breakfasts include bacon and cheese, and yoghurt and fruit. The rest of the day, choose from tortilla, lasagne, sausages, salads, vegetarian dishes. But after 11.30pm only pickled camembert-style cheese is served!

❺ V ZÁTIŠÍ
Corner of Betlémské náměstí and Liliová 1; tel: 222 221 155; www.vzatisi.cz; daily noon–3pm, 5.30–11pm; €€€
Fine-dining restaurant where Czech classics are given an exotic twist. In addition to an à la carte menu, there are 'Bohemian' and international *dégustation* menus on offer, with four courses and a range of wines.

Star of David

JOSEFOV

Walk in the footsteps of Franz Kafka around the cobbled streets of Josefov, the Jewish Quarter, visiting its historic synagogues and old cemetery, drinking up its café life, and immersing yourself in its timeless stories and atmosphere.

DISTANCE: 1.25km (1 mile)
TIME: A half day
START: Little Square
END: Spanish Synagogue
POINTS TO NOTE: The historic Jewish sites on this route are closed on Saturday.

The first Jewish community in Prague was founded in 1091. Despite periods of oppression and laws restricting Jewish residents to a small area of the city, the community nevertheless flourished, becoming a focal point for Jewish culture in Central Europe. Greater religious freedom finally came with the Age of Enlightenment and Emperor Joseph II's Patent of Toleration of 1781. The ghetto was later renamed Josephstown (Josefov) in his honour. Then in 1848 the old segregation laws were at last repealed and the Jewish community was allowed to develop freely.

One legacy of the centuries of discrimination, however, was that the quarter had never been provided with adequate sanitation. By the 1890s, the area was deemed a health hazard and almost all of it was demolished. Fortunately, the Jewish Town Hall, six synagogues and the Old Cemetery were all spared.

The community remained active until the Nazi occupation in 1939. Mass deportations began in 1941 and went on to wipe out 90 percent of the population. The Nazis intended to create a 'museum of the extinct Jewish race' here, but after the liberation it instead became the home of the largest collection of sacred Jewish artefacts in Europe. Today, Prague's Jewish community numbers around 7,000.

FRANZ KAFKA EXHIBITION

The walk starts at the Little Square (Malé náměstí – near the Astronomical Clock at the western end of the Old Town Square). Turn right off the Little Square into U Radnice and head north.

Very soon on your right at No. 5 is the block where the writer Franz Kafka was born in 1883. Little remains of the original fabric – only the stone por-

Kafka's typewriter   Decorative ceiling, Spanish Synagogue

tal – after a fire in 1887. Inside is the **Franz Kafka Exhibition ❶** (Expozice Franze Kafky; tel: 222 321 675; Tue–Fri 10am–6pm, Sat 10am–5pm), featuring photographs and manuscripts relating to the writer. For those eager to learn more, there is a more substantial museum dedicated to the writer on the Malá Strana side of the river just north of the Charles Bridge at Cihelná 2b (daily 10am–6pm).

MAISEL SYNAGOGUE

Continue north as the street becomes Maiselova to find the **Maisel Synagogue ❷** (Maiselova synagoga) on your right. This, along with the other main Jewish sites in Josefov (except the Old-New and Jerusalem synagogues) constitutes the **Jewish Museum** (www.jewishmuseum.cz; Sun–Fri Apr–Oct 9am–6pm, Nov–Mar 9am–4.30pm);

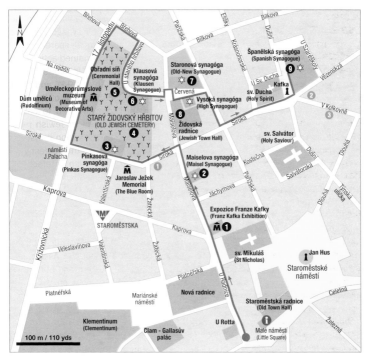

The Old Jewish Cemetery

a single ticket gains entrance to all the sites.

The Maisel Synagogue itself was founded in the 1590s by Mordecai Maisel, the wealthy mayor of the quarter, but was destroyed in 1689 when a fire gutted much of the district. The present building, its replacement, was only given its neo-Gothic appearance at the end of the 19th century. Inside is an exhibition of manuscripts, prints, textiles and liturgical silverware.

PINKAS SYNAGOGUE

At the crossroads with Široká, turn left for the **Pinkas Synagogue** ❸ (Pinkasova synagoga; part of the Jewish Museum; admission times as above), originally founded in 1479 by Rabbi Pinkas, who had fallen out with the elders of the Old-New Synagogue. The present building came into being in 1535, adapted from a house belonging to the prominent Horowitz family.

Since 1958 the synagogue has served as a memorial to 77,297 of the Czech Jewish victims of the Holocaust. The inscriptions around the interior walls list the name, date of birth and date of deportation of each victim. For many years these names were obscured – initially because of damp, then because the Communist authorities closed the synagogue, supposedly for restoration, but actually neglecting it, seemingly out of antipathy to the Jewish cause after the Six-Day War. In the 1990s, the names were carefully rewritten. A few remnants of the original wall can be seen.

Memorial

The synagogue now also serves as a memorial to the 7,500 children who died in Nazi concentration camps, and to the women who encouraged them to paint and draw while they were awaiting deportation from the holding camp at Terezín, in the Elbe Valley, approximately 60km (38 miles) to the north of Prague. The children's pictures, with their names and the dates of their death, line the walls of the first-floor gallery.

OLD JEWISH CEMETERY

The **Old Jewish Cemetery** ❹ (Starý židovský hřbitov; part of the Jewish Museum) is also accessed just nearby.

The Ceremonial Hall

Holocaust Memorial in the Pinkas Synagogue

It came into being in the 15th century, and burials continued here until 1787. The number of graves is much greater than the 12,000 gravestones would suggest – the true figure is probably closer to 100,000. Because this was the only place where Jews could be buried, graves were piled layer on layer.

The majority of the inscriptions on the stones are poetic texts of grief and mourning. The reliefs give the family name or emblem, and the profession of the deceased (scissors for a tailor, for example). The oldest monument in the cemetery is the tombstone of the poet Avigdor Kara, dating from 1439. Also buried here, in 1601, was the noted Jewish mayor Mordecai Maisel (see page 57). But the most famous tomb is that of the great scholar Rabbi Löw (1525–1609), who supposedly created the Golem (see box).

CEREMONIAL HALL

Back on Široká again, continue to the end of the street and then turn right onto 17 Listopadu. On your left, on the banks of the river, is the Rudolfinum while on your right is the Museum of Decorative Arts (closed for restoration but open for exhibitions; see page 62). Continue north, skirting the perimeter wall of the Jewish Cemetery, and turn right into Břehová and then right again into U starého hřbitova.

First on your right is the neo-Romanesque **Ceremonial Hall** ❺ (Obřadní síň; part of the Jewish Museum), built in 1911 for the Prague Burial Society, which performed charitable duties as well as burials. Inside is an exhibition devoted to Jewish life and traditions, with particular emphasis on medicine, illness and death within the ghetto.

KLAUSEN SYNAGOGUE

Next door the **Klausen Synagogue** ❻ (Klausová synagóga; part of the Jewish Museum), is a Baroque building with a long hall and barrel vaulting. It was built in 1694 to replace the little 'cells': three buildings that served as houses of prayer, classrooms and a ritual bath. It houses another part of the exhibition of Jewish customs and traditions.

OLD-NEW SYNAGOGUE

Back outside, continue to the end of the road – where it meets Maiselova – and cross over to the **Old-New Synagogue** ❼ (Staronová synagóga; www.synagogue.cz; Sun–Fri 9.30am–5pm, Apr–Oct until 6pm). This synagogue is not part of the Jewish Museum, though the modest admission charge also allows entry to the **Jerusalem Synagogue** (Apr–Oct Sun–Fri 11am–5pm).

The Old-New Synagogue dates back to the 1270s, and is the oldest Jewish house of worship still in use in Europe. It was first called the New Synagogue, but gained its present name when another synagogue – now destroyed – was built

Embroidered yarmulke (Jewish skull caps) for sale

close by. The building is an unparalleled example of a medieval two-aisled synagogue, with buttresses and a high saddle roof and brick gable (redolent of Cistercian Gothic).

The Interior

The interior is remarkably original, despite some 19th-century efforts at renovation. It had previously been left unaltered as a tribute to the 3,000 people who sought sanctuary here yet were slaughtered in the pogrom of 1389. In the vestibule are two early Baroque money boxes, used for collecting Jewish taxes from the entire kingdom. In the main aisle, between the two pillars, is the Almemor with its lectern for reading the Torah and sectioned off by a late-Gothic grille. In the middle of the east wall is the Torah shrine, called the Ark, with a triangular tympanum above. Next to the Ark is the Chief Rabbi's Chair, decorated with a Star of David. Among the other seats lining the walls is a tall one marked with a gold star. It belonged to Rabbi Löw.

Services in Hebrew are still held here on weekdays at 7.30pm, Fridays at sundown and Saturdays at 9am. The only time in its history services have not been held was during the Nazi occupation.

> ## The Golem
>
> According to legend, Rabbi Löw created a 'Golem' to defend the Jewish Quarter after Emperor Rudolf II decreed that Prague's Jews were to be expelled or killed. The Rabbi made the Golem using clay from the banks of the Vltava, and brought it to life with mystical Hebrew incantations. As the Golem grew bigger, it became more violent and started killing gentiles. Before long, the emperor rescinded his decree and the Rabbi destroyed the Golem by rubbing out the first letter of the Hebrew word *emet* ('God's truth') from the Golem's forehead to leave the word *met* ('death'). Rabbi Löw stored the monster's remains in a coffin in the attic of the Old-New Synagogue so that it could be summoned again if needed.

JEWISH TOWN HALL

Opposite the Old-New Synagogue is the **Jewish Town Hall** ❽ (Židovská radnice). It was designed in 1586 in Renaissance style by Pankratius Roder for the mayor, Mordecai Maisel, although the newest, southern part dates only from the beginning of the 20th century. In keeping with the Hebrew practice of reading from right to left, the hands on the clock tower move in an anticlockwise direction.

High Synagogue

Originally part of the Jewish Town Hall, but in 1883 given a separate entrance, is the **High Synagogue** (Vysoká synagóga), opposite the Old-New Synagogue on Červená. It is no longer open for viewing.

The ornate Moorish interior of the Spanish Synagogue

SPANISH SYNAGOGUE

Now cut through Červená to emerge onto Pařížká, an Art Nouveau boulevard of shops and restaurants. Turn right, and when you meet Široká again, either turn right again to have lunch at **King Solomon**, see ❶, or else turn left to continue the tour.

Continuing the walk eastwards, you soon encounter Jaroslav Rona's 2002 **Kafka Statue** on your left before reaching the **Spanish Synagogue** ❾ (Španělská synagóga; part of the Jewish Museum). This restored Reform synagogue was built in 1868 on the site of an earlier place of worship (older even than the Old-New Synagogue). The synagogue takes its name from the Moorish-style stucco decoration of the interior – an imitation of the style widely used in parts of Spain, including the Alhambra. On the ground floor is an exhibition on the history of the Jews in Bohemian lands from the 1780s until World War II. The first floor holds a collection of synagogue silver from Bohemia and Moravia.

On completing your Jewish cultural tour, seek out two of the area's excellent restaurants and bars: **V Kolkovně**, see ❷, and **Nostress**, see ❸, just across the road.

Food and Drink

❶ KING SOLOMON

Široká 8; tel: 224 818 752; www.kosher.cz; Sun–Thu noon–11.30pm; €€€
The only strictly kosher restaurant in Prague. Hebrew-speaking staff. Among the classic dishes of Central European Jewish cooking are chicken soup, gefilte fish, carp with prunes and duckling drumsticks with schollet and sautéed cabbage. Kosher wines are from Israel, Hungary, France and the Czech Republic. It is also possible to arrange Shabat meals beforehand and even have them delivered to your hotel (see website for details).

❷ V KOLKOVNĚ

Kolkovně 8; tel: 224 819 701; www.vkolkovne.cz; daily 11am–midnight; €€

Though located in a former printing office in a fine 19th-century building, V Kolkovně is a modern take on the traditional beer hall and is licensed from the Pilsner Urquell brewery. The decor is smart and understated (except for a slightly Captain Nemo copper-plated bar). The food is solid Czech fare – fried cheese, pork schnitzel, roast duck – and reasonably priced.

❸ NOSTRESS

V Kolkovně 9; tel: 222 317 007; www.nostress.cz; daily 10am–midnight; €€€
Stylish café-restaurant with a gallery showing contemporary photography attached. The daily lunch menus are reasonably priced (sandwiches and beer are also recommended). Dinner, however, is much more expensive. The well-executed cooking is generally of the fusion cuisine variety.

The Rudolfinum

THE RUDOLFINUM TO THE CUBISM MUSEUM

This route skirts the edge of the Old Town and provides a survey of different Czech architectural styles, from the early Gothic of the Medieval Art Gallery to the Art Nouveau Municipal House and the Cubist House of the Black Madonna.

DISTANCE: 2km (1.25 miles)
TIME: A full day
START: The Rudolfinum
END: House of the Black Madonna
POINTS TO NOTE: This route is quite art heavy, and, after two galleries, visitors might be reluctant to see a third; even so, continuing the route to the House of the Black Madonna is highly recommended. If it is any incentive, the Grand Café Orient on the first floor is a good place to rest your feet.

Start this tour of the outskirts of the Old Town at náměstí Jana Palacha. Staro-městská metro station is close by, on Kaprova; from there, turn left out of the station and walk down towards the river to enter the square.

THE RUDOLFINUM

Dominating the square is the **Rudolfi-num** ❶, an impressive neo-Renaissance building built as a concert hall from 1875

to 1884. From 1918 to 1938 it was the seat of the Czechoslovak Parliament, but after World War II it was returned to its original use as the home of the Czech Philharmonic Orchestra (www.ceskafil harmonie.cz), who regularly perform in the magnificent Dvořák Hall (see page 118). The **Galerie Rudolfinum** (www. galerierudolfinum.cz; Tue–Sun 10am–6pm, Thu until 8pm) is an important venue for the work of contemporary artists and has a lovely café.

MUSEUM OF DECORATIVE ARTS

Across the road – No.17 listopadu – from the Rudolfinum is the UPM or **Museum of Decorative Arts** ❷ (Umě-leckoprůmyslové muzeum; www.upm. cz; closed for renovation but open for exhibitions). The building dates from 1900 and is itself a fine example of the decorative arts. This is one of the most interesting museums in Prague dedicated to the history and development of decorative art and design from textiles, fashion and jewellery to glass, ceramics, wood and metal.

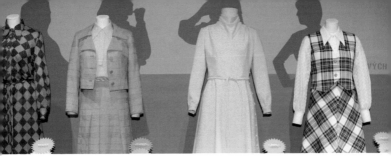

Fashion exhibits at the Museum of Decorative Arts

The collections

Each section has some wonderful items, but among the best are the collections of late 19th- and 20th-century women's costume. The collections include not only clothing but an excellent selection of shoes and accessories.

The glass and ceramics collection includes some fine examples of 16th- to 17th-century Venetian glass, but of course it is the Bohemian work that is best represented. Of the metalwork, it is probably the pieces from 1900–30 that are most interesting; look out for Josef Gočár's Cubist clock (1913). There are also fine examples of 20th-century jewellery, particularly the pieces from the 1970s and 1980s by Jozef Soukup.

The Czechs have long had a reputation for good graphic design, and this is borne out by the early 20th-century posters; chief among these are those displaying the influence of Cubism.

CUBIST ARCHITECTURE

Turn right out of the museum, along the wall of the Old Jewish Cemetery (see page 58) and then turn right into Bře-hová, which brings you out into an open square. On your left is **Les Moules**, see ❶, a good place for lunch. Cross over the wide street of Pařížská and take Bílkova, the road directly in front of you. As you leave the square look to your left along Elišky Krásnohorské and there is a **Cubist apartment block ❸** built by Otakar Novotný in 1921.

Continue to the end of the road and turn right, and at the next junction take

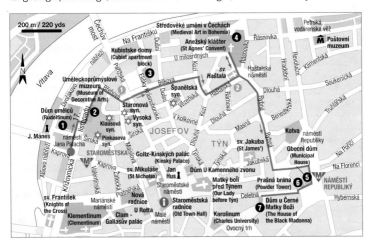

The Powder Tower

the second left into Haštalská. Here you will find a second good option for lunch, **Chez Marcel**, see ❷.

ST AGNES'S CONVENT

In front of the restaurant is the church of St Hastala, and behind this – taking the lane to the left around the church – is **St Agnes's Convent ❹** (Anežský klášter; U milosrdných 17). The convent is the first early-Gothic building in Prague, having been founded in 1234. However, the complex fell into decay and parts of it were destroyed. After many years, restorers succeeded in bringing some rooms back to their original state. These were linked to form the present-day historic complex by means of carefully reconstructed additions.

The convent buildings hold the National Gallery's collection of **Medieval Art in Bohemia and Central Europe** (Středověké uměni v Čechách; www.ngprague. cz; Tue–Sun 10am–6pm). The superb collection has been sensitively displayed and fits well into the space.

The collections

The exhibits are shown in broadly chronological order, starting with a very important early wooden statue, the *Madonna of Michle* (c.1330). Among the star exhibits are the museum's two Bohemian altarpieces: the first from Vyšší Brod (1350) and the second from Třeboň (1380–5), whose artist was one of the most important figures of the Inter-national Style. Also look out for the series from the Chapel of the Holy Cross at Karlštejn (1360–4) by Master Theodoric.

Influence from the Netherlands can be seen in later works such as Hans Pleydenwurff's *Beheading of St Barbara* (c.1470), and, at the end of the 15th century, from the Italian Renaissance in the work of the Master of Grossgmain. As well as some fabulous Swabian and Bohemian woodcarving, there are two excellent paintings by Lucas Cranach the Elder (the *Madonna of Poleň*, 1520, and *Young Lady with a Hat*, 1538). There are also fine woodcuts, notably Dürer's *Apocalypse* (1511) and *The Passion Cycle* (1509) by Cranach.

MUNICIPAL HOUSE

Now return to Haštalská and at the end of the street turn right into Rybná. Walk down Rybná, past the Modernist Hotel Josef, designed by Eva Jiřičná, to the Hotel Paříž. The short streets of Obecního domu open out into náměstí Republiky (Republic Square). Here is the Art Nouveau **Municipal House ❺** (Obecní dům; www.obecni-dum.cz; daily 10am–8pm; tours in Czech and English).

It was built in 1911 in response to the politically and economically strengthened national consciousness of the Czech bourgeoisie around the turn of the 20th century. A whole generation of artists worked on this building, including Alfons Mucha (1860–1939), who has left here some wonderful examples of his art. Every corner of the building, both inside

Municipal House   *House of the Black Madonna*

and out, is elegantly decorated, and has been carefully maintained. It was also here that the independent Czechoslovak Republic was declared in October 1918.

Today, it is home to the Prague Symphony Orchestra (www.fok.cz), which plays in the Smetana Hall (Smetanova síň). Some idea of the building's splendour can be gained in its café and restaurants.

POWDER TOWER

Adjoining the Municipal House, on Celetná, is the late-Gothic **Powder Tower** ❻ (Prašná brána; daily Apr–Sept 10am–10pm, Mar and Oct 10am–8pm, Nov–Feb 10am–6pm). It was built in the later 15th century as a city gate and acquired its name when it was used as a gunpowder storehouse; the neo-Gothic roof was added during the 19th century. It houses an exhibition 'Prague Towers' and photographs by Ladislav Sitensky. It is possible to climb the 186 steps for a fine view across the Old Town.

CZECH CUBISM EXHIBITION

Walking down Celetná brings you to the Cubist **House of the Black Madonna** ❼ (Dům u Černé Matky Boži; Ovocný trh 19; www.czkubismus.cz; Tue–Sun 10am–6pm, Tue until 7pm). The entrance is via a beautiful spiralling staircase with a Cubist motif on the bannister supports. Now under the umbrella of the Museum of Decorative Arts, the Czech Cubism Exhibition at the house is presented to combine fine arts, applied arts and architecture. Displayed over four floors above the charming Grand Café Orient, you will find works by Czech doyens of the movement, including Otto Gutfreund (1889–1927), Pavel Janák (1882–1956), Emil Filla (1882–1953), Josef Gočár (1880–1945), Jaroslav Benda (1882–1970) and Bohumil Kubišta (1884–1918). The top floor is used for workshops and educational programmes. The exhibitions throughout have fine examples of paintings, sculpture, furniture and graphic design, but the star exhibit is probably the building itself.

Food and Drink

❶ LES MOULES
Pařížká 19; tel: 222 315 022; www.les moules.cz; daily 11.30am–midnight; €€
This Belgian bar and restaurant is a good place to while away a few hours. As well as an excellent variety of Belgian beer, bottled and on tap, the food is both delicious and filling, with pride of place going to the mussels.

❷ CHEZ MARCEL
Haštalská 12; tel: 222 315 676; www.chez marcel.cz; daily 11.30am–11.30pm; no credit cards; €€
Very French, even down to the occasionally grumpy service, this bistro opposite St Agnes's Convent has all the expected dishes (steak, salads and tarte tartin), plus a few more interesting plates and French wines by the glass. Tasty, simple food.

Wenceslas Square slopes down from the National Museum

WENCESLAS SQUARE

With its Art Nouveau buildings and historic monuments, Wenceslas Square has witnessed the proclamation of independence in 1918, the Prague Spring in 1968 and the Velvet Revolution in 1989.

DISTANCE: 2.5km (1.5 miles)
TIME: 2 hours
START: National Museum
END: Museum of Communism
POINTS TO NOTE: The nearest metro station to this route's starting point is Muzeum, at the intersection of lines A and C.

Wenceslas Square (Václavské náměstí) is actually more of a broad boulevard than an open square. Sloping down for almost half a mile at the heart of Nové Město (New Town), its wide pedestrian zones follow the course of the fortifications that surrounded the city in the Middle Ages, before Charles IV erected the New Town in a semicircle around the old.

History of the square
Although the square was originally used as a horse market, it eventually became the setting for much grander events. All Prague's historic uprisings – from the Reformationist Hussite Rebellion in the early 15th century to the nationalist riots in 1848 to the remarkably peaceful Velvet Revolution in 1989 – have focused on the square.

In 1918, crowds assembled here for the proclamation of independence for Czechoslovakia. Then, in March 1939, the Nazis took that independence away again and celebrated their bloodless conquest with a military parade here. In 1968, Soviet tanks rolled into the square to crush the Prague Spring and with it, Alexander Dubček's aspirations for 'socialism with a human face'. Finally, in 1989 the square was the rallying point for the series of demonstrations that led to the Velvet Revolution and the country's independence.

The square today
Since those heady days, however, the square has lost some of its lustre. Fast-food chains, casinos, strip clubs, sausage stalls and parked cars have set the tone. But the city authorities are waking up to the need for renewal. Green spaces and pedestrian zones have been reintegrated with the square

Wenceslas Square at dusk

and traffic re-routed to a city ring road. High-end stores now blend with tacky souvenir shops and the notorious sausage stalls littering the square are making way for flower stands. Wenceslas Square is set to get an even bigger facelift, though exactly when is a point of contention.

NATIONAL MUSEUM

The route begins at the southern end of the square, in front of the old **National Museum ❶** (Národní muzeum; www. nm.cz). Constructed in 1890 to designs by Josef Schulz, this neo-Renaissance palace is currently closed for renovations that will double the exhibition space inside. It is due to reopen in the summer of 2018.

In front of the museum, look out for two small mounds in the cobbled pavement. These mark the place where a Czech student named Jan Palach set himself on fire in January 1969 in protest against Soviet oppression. A month later, another student, Jan Zajíc, did the same.

Just to the east of the old National Museum, along Wilsonova (named after President Wilson, who, after World War I, championed the principle of self-determination that led to the independence of Czechoslovakia) is the old **Stock Exchange building** (Vinohradská 1). This was transformed into a glass structure to house the Federal Assembly between 1966 and 1972, and subsequently housed Radio Free Europe, broadcasting US propaganda to Muslim Fundamentalist audiences. Since 2009 it has been taken over by the National Museum and now houses the **New Building** (Nová budova; www. nm.cz; daily 10am–6pm), host to temporary exhibitions.

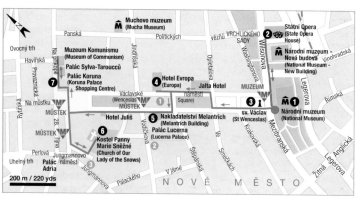

A performance at the State Opera

STATE OPERA HOUSE

Just beyond it is the **State Opera House** ❷ (Státní Opera; www.narodni-divadlo. cz; closed for restoration until September 2018; see page 118), built in 1888 and renowned for having one of the most beautiful auditoriums in Central Europe. Among the famous conductors and singers to have worked here are Gustav Mahler, Richard Strauss, Nellie Melba and Benjamino Gigli. The theatre's reputation was greatly enhanced under the stewardships of Alexander Zemlinksy (1911–27) and Georg Szell (1927–38), who staged works by their contemporaries, Krenek, Hindemith and Schreker.

Beyond the opera house is the city's **main railway station** (Hlavní nádraží), with an Art Nouveau structure and Communist-era additions.

STATUE OF ST WENCESLAS

Back on Wenceslas Square, in front of the old National Museum, is the equestrian **Statue of St Wenceslas** ❸ by Josef Myslbek, erected in this commanding position in 1912 after 30 years of planning and design. The base, designed by Alois Dryák, depicts saints Agnes, Adelbert, Procopius and Ludmila (Wenceslas's grandmother). It was from here that Alois Jirásek read the proclamation of Czechoslovakian independence to the assembled crowds on 28 October 1918. A less happy event, though, is memorialised a little way down from the statue, in the form of a headstone featuring the images of student martyrs Palach and Zajíc.

NUCLEAR FALLOUT BUNKER

Continue the walk along the right-hand side of the square and you will soon arrive at the **Jalta Hotel** (No 45; www. hoteljalta.com), which from the 1950s harboured a big secret: hidden under the hotel is a communist-era nuclear bunker. Built to hold 150 people, it has massive reinforced walls to provide shelter for prominent officials and distinguished officers for as long as two months if war broke out. The Ministry of Defence owned the bunker until it was declassified in 1997. Now the property of the hotel, tours (booked in advance) are available, led by a guide in a period security police uniform – highlights include the comms room, where wiretaps in the bedrooms of important guests were monitored.

ART NOUVEAU ARCHITECTURE

A bit further on is the magnificent **Hotel Evropa** ❹, at Nos 25–7. This grand Art Nouveau establishment is the result of architect Alois Dryák's makeover of the building in 1905 (with the assistance of architectural sculptor Ladislav Šaloun).

Melantrich Building
Make a pit-stop at the converted tram café, **Café Tramvaj 11**, see ❶, on the central reservation before crossing to

the other side of the square and the **Melantrich Building** ❺ (Nakladatelství Melantrich; built 1914) at No. 36. It was on the balcony here on 24 November 1989 that Alexander Dubček and Václav Havel appeared together before a crowd of 300,000 people in a pivotal event of the Velvet Revolution. The building is now occupied by Marks & Spencer. Just nearby, at No. 34, is the Wiehl House, built in 1896 to designs by Antonín Wiehl. Its extravagant facade is decorated with neo-Renaissance murals by Czech artist Mikuláš Aleš and others.

Lucerna Palace shopping arcade

Tucked away behind, in the block between Štěpánská and Vodičkova, is the labyrinthine **Lucerna Palace** (Palác Lucerna) shopping arcade. This Art Nouveau complex harbours the gorgeous **Lucerna cinema** (operating since 1909) as well as a grand concert hall and several cafés – including the **Lucerna**, see ❷. Hanging from the ceiling of the atrium by the cinema is David Černy's amusing sculpture of King Wenceslas on his upside-down horse, a satire on the monumental version in the square outside.

Aficionados of Art Nouveau and in particular the work of Czech artist Alphonse Mucha, should take a detour to the Muchovo museum (www.mucha.cz; daily 10am–6pm), on Panská parallel with Wenceslas Square.

King Wenceslas on his upside-down horse

MODERNIST ARCHITECTURE

Out in the fresh air again, continue your walk down the square, passing Ludvík Kysela's **Alfa Palace** at No. 28 and Pavel Janák's **Hotel Juliš** at No. 22 – both 1920s Modernist affairs. At No. 12 is a brief Art Nouveau diversion, the **Peterka House**, built to Jan Kotěra's designs in 1899–1900. At No. 6 is the 1929 Functionalist building designed by Ludvík Kysela for Tomáš Bat'a, art patron, progressive industrialist and founder of the shoe empire.

OUR LADY OF THE SNOWS

When you come to Kysela's Palác Astra (former Lindt Building) at No. 4, turn left into the passageway through the middle

Our Lady of the Snows

to emerge on the other side in Jungmannovo náměstí. Look out for the memorial to Josef Jungmann (1773–1847), who revived the Czech language. On your left, outside the gate of the Franciscan rectory, is a **Cubist lamppost**, designed by Emil Králíček in 1913. Behind this is the **Church of Our Lady of the Snows** ❻ (Kostel Panny Marie Sněžné; www.pms.ofm.cz; daily 9am–5.30pm; free), which can be accessed via a gateway around the corner.

History

Completed in 1347, the church was planned as a coronation church by Charles IV. The designs envisaged a three-aisled Gothic cathedral church and the tallest building in Prague. However, shortage of money and the start of the Hussite Wars meant the plans were never fulfilled. In fact, it was from here that the radical Hussites marched to the New Town Hall in 1419 in order to teach the city's officials a lesson, in one of Prague's infamous defenestrations (see page 44).

The interior

Today, all that can be seen of Charles IV's grand plan is the out-of-proportion chancel with its extravagant black-and-gold Baroque altarpiece. The painting on the altar (by an unknown Italian artist) depicts the legend of Our Lady of the Snows. In the 4th century AD, the Virgin Mary appeared in a Roman merchant's dream and told him to build a temple on the place where snow would be found the following morning. When he woke up the next morning, the merchant was confused, since it was the middle of summer. Even so, he went out and found that the Esquiline hill was covered in snow. Following the request, he had the Church of St Maria Maggiore built on the site.

If you are ready for lunch at this point, **Lahůdky Zlatý Kříž** is a fine Czech delicatessen just round the corner on Jungmannova, see ❸.

SHOPPING

After lunch, retrace your steps to Wenceslas Square, cross over, and at the other corner you will find the monumental **Koruna Palace Shopping Centre** ❼

(Palác Koruna). Built in 1914 to designs by Antonín Pfeiffer and Matěj Blecha, it shows early hints of Modernism.

Outside again, the street that runs perpendicular to Wenceslas Square is Na Příkopě ('On the Moat'); it was originally built on top of a river (filled in in 1760) that separated the walls of Staré Město and Nové Město. Now an upmarket shopping street, it follows the line of the old fortifications all the way down to the Gothic Powder Tower at náměstí Republiky (see page 65).

At No.10 Na Příkopě is the **Museum of Communism** (Muzeum Komunismu; www.muzeumkomunismu.cz; daily 9am–9pm) devoted to the Communist era (1948–89). Exhibits include propaganda

posters, a mock-up of a class-room of the era, and a sinister interrogation room.

The walk ends here. And if you wish to catch the metro, backtrack to take the escalators down to Můstek Station, at the intersection of lines A and B. 'Můstek' means 'little bridge', and as you descend you will see illuminated the stone remains of what was once a bridge that connected the fortifications of Prague's Old and New Towns. When workers were building the station a few decades ago, they had to be inoculated against the tuberculosis bacteria uncovered by their excavations. The bacteria had lain here dormant, encased in horse manure, since the Middle Ages.

Food and Drink

① CAFÉ TRAMVAJ 11

Václavské náměstí 32; daily 9am–midnight, from 10am Sun; €€€

If you don't mind paying a bit more for a coffee or light bite to get away from the usual chains, these two converted historic trams placed in the middle of the square offer a delightful atmospheric setting. Seating inside or outside.

② KAVÁRNA LUCERNA

Vodičkova 36 (pasáž U Nováků); tel: 224 215 495; daily 10am–midnight; €

This stylish café is a welcome spot to hang out over a cup of coffee, glass of wine or

snack while taking in the architectural charms of the Art Nouveau passage where it resides. Live music on the weekends.

③ LAHŮDKY ZLATÝ KŘÍŽ

Jungmannova 34; tel: 222 519 451; www.lahudkyzlatykriz.cz; Mon–Fri 6.30am–7pm, Sat 9am–3pm; €

Follow the stream of locals from the square to this nondescript shop on a side street. Inside, behold a delicatessen classic where you are served from refrigerated counters rammed full of typical Czech snack food. Bread is loaded up with ham or salami or maybe smoked salmon, with a dollop or two of cream cheese or potato salad on top, and maybe a gherkin garnish or a little caviar.

'Fred and Ginger' close-up

NOVÉ MĚSTO

This route explores the artistic legacy of the Czech nationalist struggle through Prague's National Theatre and one of its greatest composers, Antonín Dvořák, as well as some interesting modern architecture.

DISTANCE: 2.5km (1.5 miles)
TIME: A half day
START: National Theatre
END: Dvořák Museum
POINTS TO NOTE: A varied walk that takes you from the river bank into the heart of the New Town's university district.

Prague's 'New Town' has a very different feel to the narrow streets of Staré Město (Old Town; see page 48) or Malá Strana (Lesser Town; see page 40). The grand 19th-century buildings conceal little gems, such as a Functionalist building for an artists' association, Gothic cloisters and a lovely botanical garden.

NATIONAL THEATRE

Begin your walk at the **National Theatre** ❶ (Národní divadlo; see page 118), a fine reminder of the nation's enthusiasm for culture in the late 19th century. In 1845 the Estates, with their German majority, turned down the request for a Czech theatre. In response, money was collected

on a voluntary basis, and the building of a Czech theatre declared a national duty. In 1852 the site was bought, and the foundation stone was laid in 1868.

The building was designed by Josef Zítek in a style reminiscent of the Italian Renaissance. The theatre was completed by 1881 but then destroyed in a fire just before it was due to open. Undeterred, Czechs of all classes from all over the country once more contributed their coins to the rebuilding fund, and within nine months reconstruction could begin. Under Josef Schulz's direction, using many notable artists including Vojtěch Hynais, it was completed and opened in 1883 with a performance of Smetana's *Libuše*.

MODERNIST ARCHITECTURE

Head upstream along the river on Masarykovo nábřeží. On your right you will pass the wooded **Slavic Island** ❷ (Slovanský ostrov), home to the Žofín concert hall (www.zofin.cz), where famous composers such as Berlioz, Liszt and Wagner have conducted. It now also

Café Slavia   *National Theatre*

hosts conferences and events. At the far end of the island is the **Mánes House**, an excellent example of Functionalist architecture. It was built to designs by Otakar Novotný between 1927 and 1930 for the Mánes Artists' Association and now houses temporary exhibitions.

'Fred and Ginger' building

Masarykovo nábřeží takes you to the Jirásek Bridge (Jiráskův most). Opposite the bridge, on the corner of Resslova, is Frank Gehry and Vlado Milunič's Nationale Nederlanden Administrative Building, or **Tančící dům ❸**. Also nicknamed the 'Fred and Ginger' building on account of its supposed likeness to a dancing couple, it was built in 1992–6 and, now the novelty has worn off, its faults have become apparent; it wasn't well finished and the quirky design now seems like postmodern grandstanding. Its rooftop restaurant, **Ginger & Fred**, see ❶, offers wonderful views over the city.

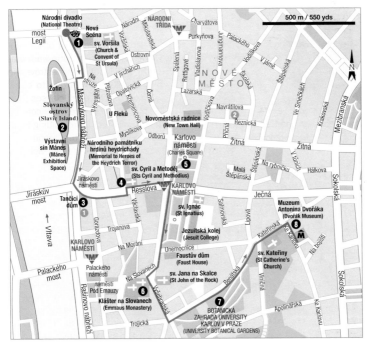

Emmaus Monastery

NATIONAL MEMORIAL

Walk up Resslova and on your left is the Orthodox **Church of SS Cyril and Methodius** (Kostel sv. Cyrila a Metoděje). The church is usually closed, but you can see through the windows in the porch into the ornate Baroque interior. Below, in the crypt is the **National Memorial to the Heroes of the Heydrich Terror ❹** (Národního památníku hrdinů heydrichády; www.pamatnik-heydrichiady.cz; Tue–Sun Mar–Oct 9am–5pm, Nov–Feb closed Sun; free). A number of photographs, documents and a plaque on display tell the story of the seven members of the resistance who held out here after succeeding in assassinating Richard Heydrich, the brutal Nazi governor, on 17 May 1942. When the hiding place was discovered they shot themselves rather than surrender to the SS. The Nazis exacted revenge: on 10 June 1942 Heydrich's successor ordered the village of Lidice to be burnt to the ground. All the men were shot and the women and children deported to concentration camps.

CHARLES SQUARE

At the top of Resslova is **Charles Square ❺** (Karlovo náměstí), which was laid out during the construction of the New Town and was once the site of a cattle market.

Faust House
On the right, south of some well-tended gardens, is the **Faust House**. According to legend, this was once the residence of the German magician and alchemist Dr Faustus, famed for selling his soul to the devil in exchange for power and knowledge, but it was in fact the home of English adventurer Edward Kelly, who promised Emperor Rudolf II a precious lump of gold from his alchemical laboratory. This he singularly failed to do and ended his life in one of the king's dungeons.

If you still have not eaten then try **Miyabi**, see ❷, which is on Navrátilova off Vodičkova at the top left-hand corner of the square.

EMMAUS MONASTERY

To continue on your way, take Vyšehradská, south of the square to reach the **Emmaus Monastery ❻** (Klášter na Slovanech; www.emauzy.cz; Mon–Sat 11am–5.30pm). Owing to a location that controls access to the Vltava River, it has played a significant role in the city since it was founded by Charles IV in 1347.

A misconceived American bombing raid during World War II – the hapless pilots thought they were over Dresden, although that is no excuse – destroyed many of the monastery's irreplaceable medieval art treasures, but the magnificent cloisters alone make the place well worth a visit. The original Gothic towers were destroyed in the attack but replaced in 1968 by the distinctive, overlapping concrete curves, topped with 1.3kg (nearly 3lbs) of gold. The two sail-shaped buttresses are considered to be one of the city's most striking pieces of modern architecture.

Art Nouveau building detail

Dvořák Museum

BOTANICAL GARDENS

At the bottom of Vyšehradská, past the Baroque Church of St John on the Rock, is the **University Botanical Gardens** ❼ (Botanická Zahrada University Karlov v Praze; www.bz-uk.cz; daily Apr–Aug 10am–7.30pm, Sept–Mar 10am–6pm, Nov–Jan 10am–4pm; free but charge for the glasshouse). First set out in 1897, the gardens remain a delight to this day; all the specimens are well labelled and the gardens are dotted with modern sculptures. The winding paths, rockeries and pools mean there are lots of quiet nooks and crannies to explore. The highlight is a beautiful series of restored pre-war greenhouses, dripping with tropical vegetation and including a delightful lily pond.

DVOŘÁK MUSEUM

After leaving the gardens take Benátská, the road leading up the hill past a number of university buildings. At the top take Kateřinská and turn right into Ke Karlovu. Here is the Villa Amerika, home to the **Dvořák Museum** ❽ (Muzeum Antonína Dvořáka; www.nm.cz; Tue–Sun 10am–1.30pm, 2–5pm), which honours one of the greatest Czech composers (1841–1904). This delightful little building, named after a 19th-century inn and designed by Kilián Ignaz Dientzenhofer, was built in 1720 as a summer palace for the Michna family. The Michnas of Vacínov were an important noble family in Bohemia during the Habsburg era. As Catholics, they rose to prominence after the Hussite defeat at the Battle of the White Mountain in 1620. At one time they owned the huge castle of Konopiště and as well as employing Kilián Ignaz Dientzenhofer they commissioned buildings from the Italian architect Carlo Lurago.

The museum contains various Dvořák memorabilia, including his Bösendorfer piano and his viola, as well as displays of photographs and facsimiles of letters, tickets and manuscripts. The first floor is beautifully decorated with Johann Ferdinand Schor's wonderful frescoes depicting classical mythology themes.

Food and Drink

❶ GINGER & FRED

Rašínovo nábřeží; tel: 221 984 160; www.ginger-fred-restaurant.cz; daily 11.30am–midnight; €€€
Formal restaurant at the top of the 'Fred and Ginger' building offering panoramic views and French and international dishes. There is an à la carte menu, but also a reasonably priced set-lunch menu.

❷ MIYABI

Navrátilova 10; tel: 296 233 102; www.miyabi.cz; Mon–Sat 11.30am–11pm; €€€
For a change from pork and dumplings, try this charming Japanese restaurant. The menu includes everything from sushi to bento boxes and noodles, soups and rice dishes. There is also a fine selection of teas.

Statues at Vyšehrad Cemetery

VYŠEHRAD

According to legend this is where it all started: Vyšehrad was the rock on which Libuše and Přemysl founded the city. Today it is a site of nationalist pride and noted as the burial ground of many famous Czechs.

DISTANCE: 1km (0.5 mile)
TIME: A half day
START: Vyšehrad metro station
END: Hodek House
POINTS TO NOTE: While it is easier to take the metro to the starting point, it is also possible to take a pleasant walk along the embankment of the River Vltava to reach Vyšehrad. Continue on from the Jirásek Bridge on route 9, and you will reach Vyšehrad in about 10 minutes.

Vyšehrad is a rocky hill that rises from the place where the Vltava reaches the old city limits. According to legend it was here, in her father's castle, that Princess Libuše had her vision of the golden city of Prague: 'I see a great city, whose fame will reach to the stars… there in the woods you shall build your castle and your settlement, which shall be named Praha.' Archaeologists doubt the veracity of this tale: Prague Castle was built in the 9th century, while Vyšehrad was erected in the 10th. But in the second half of the 19th century, at the peak of the Czech national revival, the story was irresistible to the likes of Smetana and Mendelssohn, and it formed the basis of their operas *Libuše* and *Libussa's Prophecy*.

Vyšehrad (literally 'high castle') has played a key role in Prague's history since the Přemyslid kings established it as their seat of power. Its tumultuous career as a battle fortress began in 1004, when it repelled the invading forces of Poland's Boleslav the Brave. Over the years the royal residence alternated between Vyšehrad and Hradčany, and the hill was repeatedly ransacked by foreign armies. Today, by contrast, the monuments of Vyšehrad are set in attractive parkland.

TÁBOR GATE

Begin the walk at **Vyšehrad metro station ❶** and take the steps that lead towards the imposing Communist-built Congress Centre (Kongresové Centrum), formerly known as the Palace

Church of SS Peter and Paul   *Jan Neruda grave, Vyšehrad Cemetery*

of Culture. Walk in front of the centre and descend the short flight of stairs onto Na Bučance and follow the signposts that lead towards Vyšehrad. Carry straight on past **Fine Cafe**, see ❶, below the 14th-century ramparts (a good place to refresh yourself before the sightseeing ahead) and turn right into the **Tábor Gate ❷** (Táborská brána).

Just beyond the gate is the **Information Centre of the Vyšehrad National Cultural Monument** (Vyšehrad Národní Kulturní Památka; www.praha-vysehrad.cz; daily Apr–Oct 9.30am–6pm, Nov–Mar 9.30am–5pm; charge for exhibitions on the site) housed in the remains of the Špička Gate.

ST MARTIN'S ROTUNDA

Ahead is the 17th-century Leopold Gate and, to the right, **St Martin's Rotunda**

❸ (Rotunda sv. Martina; open only for mass). This is a tiny Romanesque church dating from the 11th century, sensitively restored in the 1870s, and one of the oldest churches in the country, alongside St George's Basilica in Hradčany (see page 30)

DEVIL'S PILLAR

From here, take a left onto K Rotunde, with its low stone walls. Along this quiet street you'll pass a lawn. where three short stone columns lean against each other at odd angles. This is the **Devil's Pillar**. It is said that a priest bet the devil that he could say mass before the devil could deliver a column from St Peter's Basilica in Rome. The devil took a column from a closer church, but St Peter intervened, waylaying the devil and breaking the pillar in three.

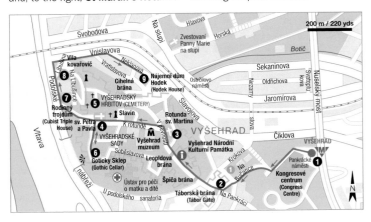

Cubist Triple House

VYŠEHRAD PARK

Further on is the well-tended **Vyšehrad Park** and the **Church of SS Peter and Paul** ❹ (Kostel sv. Petra a Pavla; tel: 224 911 353; daily Apr–Oct 10am–6pm, Sept–Mar 10am–5pm, opens 10.30am Sun), which has Art Nouveau paintings of the saints. There has been a church here since the 11th century, but today's twin-spired neo-Gothic edifice hails from 1885.

VYŠEHRAD CEMETERY

Nearby lies the 1870 **Vyšehrad Cemetery** ❺ (Vyšehradský hřbitov; tel: 274 774 835; May–Sept 8am–7pm Mar–Apr, Oct until 6pm, Nov–Feb until 5pm; free), the resting place of national figures including composers Smetana and Dvořák, writers Jan Neruda and Karel Čapek, and artist Alfons Mucha. A large monument, the Slavín, honours them all.

Legendary statues

Pass through the stone gate opposite the cemetery and you will enter a wide lawn graced with four monumental statues by Jan Myslbek, depicting characters from Czech legends, including Libuše. Further along is the summer palace of Charles IV. Also here is the **Gothic Cellar** ❻, with a permanent exhibition on the history of the site. There is lovely view over the river and the city from the battlements. The remnants of buildings jutting out of the rock were once the outpost towers from which sentinels kept watch over the Vltava.

To descend to the embankment, return to the road in front of the cemetery and, near the medallion to the geologist Jan Krejčí, take the precipitous steps on the western side of the hill to the Vltava.

CUBIST HOUSES

On the way down you pass above a splendid Cubist house by architect Josef Chochol (1880–1956): the **Cubist Triple House** ❼ (Rodinný trojdům), built in 1914, soon after which Chochol abandoned Cubism and worked in the Functionalist style.

At the bottom of the steps, on the corner of the Rašínovo nábřeží and Libušina, and nearby on Neklavova, are two more Chochol wonders, the **Villa Kovařovič** ❽ (1913) and the **Hodek House** ❾ (Nájemní dům Hodek; 1914). Both fit graceful facades into corner sites, the latter dramatically projecting from the hillside.

You can catch tram No. 17 back to the city centre from outside the villa.

Food and Drink

❶ **FINE CAFE**
Lumirova 33; tel: 725 605 041;
www.finecafe.cz; Mon–Fri 7.30am–
9.30pm, Sat–Sun 8am–9.30pm; €
A pleasant modern café serving
Mediterranean fare, perfect for a late
breakfast or brunch. Light lunches include
wraps, salads and soups, with pasta and
grills for a heartier meal.

Franz Kafka's grave in the New Jewish Cemetery

VINOHRADY AND ŽIŽKOV

Cemeteries, futuristic design and nationalist dreams all combine to give this journey through a couple of Prague's lesser-known but nonetheless fascinating areas a sense of discovery and adventure.

DISTANCE: 5km (3 miles)
TIME: A full day
START: New Jewish Cemetery
END: Museum of the City of Prague
POINTS TO NOTE: The first part of this route is best taken by public transport – it would turn into quite a trek otherwise. Buy a 24-hour ticket that allows you to use the metro and trams for a whole day.

This route explores two of Prague's more interesting outer districts, the first the sometimes down-at-heel district of apartment blocks that is Žižkov (also known as Prague 3). Its working-class credentials are well established and it was at one time a hotbed of sedition. It is also famous for a huge number of local pubs (more than any other district of Prague), not all of which are welcoming or salubrious. The neighbouring district of Vinohrady gets its name from the vineyards that once thrived here. Today, in contrast to Žižkov, it is rather bourgeois, pleasant, and lively – full of young, upwardly mobile Czechs, who live in the *fin-de-siècle* apartment blocks that make up much of the area.

ŽIŽKOV'S CEMETERIES

Begin at the far-flung end of Žižkov by the **New Jewish Cemetery ❶** (Židovské Hřbitovy; www.synagogue.cz; Mon–Thu and Sun Apr–Sept 9am–5pm, Oct–Mar 9am–4pm, Fri 9am–2pm all year; male visitors must wear yarmulkes, skull caps, available from the gatehouse; free). The cemetery is easily reached by metro, alighting at Želivského station, or take the tram (Nos 10, 11, 16 and 26 all stop here). It is a serene and atmospheric spot with attractive, tree-lined avenues of graves overgrown with ivy. Looking at the headstones you realise just how wealthy and important the local Jewish community was before World War II. It included owners of industry, doctors and lawyers, and, ironically, many were German-speakers (most of the inscriptions are in either Hebrew or German).

Many people visit to see the grave of Franz Kafka, usually covered in flowers and notes (follow the signs leading

Church of the Sacred Heart

to block 21). However, the plain Cubist headstone is not the most impressive; look instead for the striking Art Nouveau peacock on the headstone of painter Max Horb (in block 19).

Olšany Cemetery

Leave the New Jewish Cemetery and take either the metro to Flóra station, or tram 10, 11 or 16 to the stop of the same name. Here you will find the second of Žižkov's large cemeteries, **Olšany ❷** (Hřbitov Olšanske; May–Sept 8am–7pm, Mar–Apr, Oct 8am–6pm, Nov–Feb 8am–5pm; free). This huge necropolis has been the preferred burial spot of many famous Czechs (particularly if they have not managed to get a spot in Vyšehrad). Wonderfully Gothic

in parts, it has higgledy piggledy graves, all slightly overgrown. Among the famous Czechs buried here are painter Josef Mánes (1784–1843), Art Nouveau Symbolist sculptor František Bílek (1872–1941) and painter and writer Josef Lada (1887–1957).

However, perhaps the most venerated grave is that of Jan Palach (1948–69), who committed suicide in political protest in 1969 and whose body was moved here in 1990. Palach is buried near the main entrance on Vinohradská. Also here is what must be one of the most overblown funerary monuments, that of Rodina Hrdličkova: a sculptural group with a woman pleading with a man in uniform not to follow an angel up to heaven.

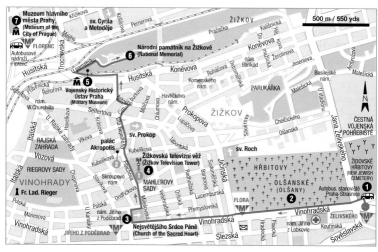

Prague Television Tower

Close-up of the 'babies' on the Television Tower

CHURCH OF THE SACRED HEART

Time to get back on public transport, this time to Jiříhoz Poděbrad by metro or on the tram (again Nos 10, 11 or 16). On the square of the same name as the metro station is the most unusual Modernist building to be found in Prague, the **Church of the Sacred Heart** ❸ (Nejsvětějšího Srdce Páně; www.srdce pane.cz; only open 40 mins before and 30 mins after mass, Mon–Sat 8am, 6pm, Sun 9am, 11am, 6pm; free). Designed by the architect Josip Plečnik (who was responsible for the restoration of St Vitus), it was built in 1932 in an eclectic style, which looks forward to the later developments of postmodernism. The monolithic structure uses elements of Classical and Egyptian styles on a rather uncompromising exterior, and is impressive but not immediately appealing. However, it is enlivened by the huge glass clock on the narrow tower flanked by obelisks.

Unlike the forbidding facade, the interior is high and spacious with a coffered ceiling. The clock tower is climbed via a ramp that is double-sided so that the light streams through from one side of the tower to the other; peering out through the glass faces gives a spectacular view over the city.

TELEVISION TOWER

Retrace your steps to the square and this time continue on foot, taking Mile-šovská at the northeast corner. This leads to Mahlerovy sady (Mahler Park) where, dominating the entire district and much of the city, is the **Žižkov Television Tower** ❹ (Žižkovska televizní věž; www.towerpark.cz; daily 8am–midnight). At 216 metres (708ft) and with a boldly modern (almost science-fiction-inspired) design based on three interlocked towers, this is the most adventurous piece of architecture (by Václav Aulický and Jiří Kozák) of the Communist era. Inspired by the similar tower on Alexanderplatz in Berlin, in an unpopular move it was built on the site of an old Jewish cemetery (used between 1786 and 1890). It is the tallest building in Prague.

Work began on construction in 1985, and the finishing touches were only made in 1991 after the fall of the Communist regime; before then it had allegedly been used for blocking foreign broadcasts from the West. Since then the tower has acquired a number of rather alien babies crawling up the steel tubes, courtesy of David Černý.

It is possible to take the lift up to the Observatory at 93 metres (305ft), from where there is an awe-inspiring view over the entire city with telescopes provided. After a major renovation there are now three cabins, each with a different theme and unique perspective of the city, plus a room to view a film of the history of the tower. For dining in the sky the **Oblaca Restaurant** and café offers some tremendous views, see ❶.

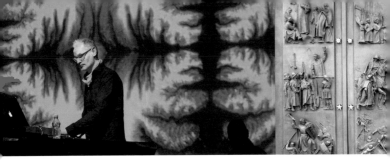
The Acropolis Palace hosts an eclectic programme

Acropolis Palace

Easily visible from the tower (looking north) is a colourful apartment block on the nearby corner of Kubelíkova and Víta nejedléno. This is the **Acropolis Palace** (palác Akropolis; www.palacakropolis.cz; box office Mon–Fri 10am–midnight, Sat–Sun 4pm–midnight), an arts centre set in the pre-war Akropolis theatre. The centre has a concert hall, cinema, theatre and exhibition space. Notable for putting on an eclectic selection of groups and acts, especially world music performers, this is one of Prague's more exciting music venues. Be sure not to miss the wonderfully designed bar and **restaurant** either: see ❷.

ŽIŽKOV HILL

Make your way down the hill taking Víta nejedléno and Cimburkovo, turn left into Štítného and then go down Jeronýmova on to the main road of Husitská. Turn left, cross the road and just before you reach the railway bridge take the cobbled road U památníku on the right.

Military Museum

On the way up the hill you will pass the **Military Museum** ❺ (Vojenský Historický Ústav Praha; U Památníku 2; www.vhu.cz; Tue–Sun 10am–6pm; free), which is rather more interesting than first impressions might suggest. The exhibits tell the story of the Czechoslovak Army from its inception in 1918 up to World War II and, apart from an impressive collection of headgear, there are good displays on World Wars I and II.

NATIONAL MEMORIAL

Keep on climbing through the wooded park and you will come to a series of steps that lead up Vítkov Hill to a wide esplanade. Here you will find the **National Memorial** ❻ (Národní památník; www.nm.cz; Wed–Sun 10am–6pm), an immense granite-faced cube containing the Tomb of the Unknown Soldier.

Right in front of it stands one of the biggest equestrian statues in the world, the monument to the Hussite leader Jan Žižka. The enormous equestrian statue (given greater height by being placed on a granite platform), by the Czech sculptor Bohumil Kafka (1878–1942), was commissioned after a competition in 1925 (one of a series that had created bad feeling and controversy about how to commemorate Žižka's victory). Only the Stalin monument, which had dominated Letná Hill until it was demolished in 1963, was bigger than that of Žižka.

The granite monolith of the National Memorial itself was initially designed by Jan Zázvorka and built in 1929–30. However, after World War II the building was redesigned and used as both the Tomb of the Unknown Soldier and as a final resting place of worthies of

National Memorial doors

Statue of Jan Žižkov at the National Memorial

the Communist Party, including Klement Gottwald, whose body was preserved in a similar way to that of Lenin in Red Square in Moscow. Gottwald is now in Olšany Cemetery (see page 80). Although it is not possible to gain access at present, the legacy of the Communist redesign can be seen in the numerous reliefs and statues of heroic workers and revolutionary soldiers that adorn the bronze doors.

The complex now has an air of slight neglect, and there are few other places in Prague where the ghost of the Communist years can be felt so easily. However, the walk up through the park is pleasant and the views from the top of the hill are wonderful.

To get back into town, retrace your steps down the hill and turn left into Husitská. At the first bus stop you come to (on U památníku), catch either the No. 175 to Florenc, or No. 133 to Staroměstská.

CITY OF PRAGUE MUSEUM

Those who still have some energy left should alight at Florenc and make their way to Na Poříčí 51 and the **Museum of the City of Prague** ❼ (Muzeum hlavního města Prahy; tel: 224 816 772; www.muzeumprahy.cz; Tue–Sun 9am–6pm), a fascinating collection housed in an imposing building. Much of the labelling is in Czech only, so ask to borrow the English booklet from the front desk.

The collection

The galleries take you through the history of the city in great depth, from prehistory and the medieval period on the ground floor, to the Renaissance and Baroque upstairs. The museum's prize exhibit is undoubtably Antonín Langweil's enormous paper model of the city (1837). Also here is the architect Josef Mánes's original design for the astrological face of the Old Town Hall.

Food and Drink

❶ OBLACA RESTAURANT

Malhlerovy Sady 1; tel: 210 320 086; www.towerpark.cz; daily 8am–midnight; €€€

A sleek modern restaurant some 66m (216ft) above the ground in the Žižkov Television Tower, which serves modern cuisine using local seasonal ingredients. There are great views to accompany dishes such as saddle of suckling pig and fillet of Czech trout. It's expensive but there is also a café serving lighter snacks.

❷ PALÁC AKROPOLIS RESTAURACE

Kubelíkova 1548/27; tel: 296 330 990; Mon–Thu 11am–12.30am, Fri–Sun 11am–1.30am; €

The food is simple but tasty, and you can drink here till late, but the surreal decor is the real star. Created by artist František Skála, it features an aquarium full of bizarre objects and even an upside-down canoe.

Modern art at the National Gallery

MUSEUM OF MODERN ART

The district of Holešovice started as a farming hamlet, then later, in 1884, was incorporated into Prague as an industrial suburb. Today, however, it is a fixture on the tourist map by virtue of its art museum.

DISTANCE: 0.8km (0.5 mile) not including distance at the museum
TIME: 2–3 hours
START: Vltavská metro station
END: Veletržní Palace
POINTS TO NOTE: The museum is closed on Monday. Trams 6, 12 and 17 and the metro serve Holešovice.

Emerging from the main exit of the shabby metro station of Vltavská, turn right (west) and walk up Antonínská (crossing over Bubenská) to Holešovice district's main square, Strossmayerovo náměstí. On your left is the large **Church of St Antony ❶** while the cobbled square in front forms the meeting point for several major tram lines. From the end of the square, turn right onto Dukelských hrdinů and walk down the hill, perhaps stopping for a cream cake at **Liberské Lahůdky** on the way, see ❶. After a few minutes you come to the art museum on your left at No. 47. Just before you go in, look further down the hill and you can see in the distance the Průmyslový Palace.

ART MUSEUM

The **Veletržní Palace ❷** (Veletržní palác; www.ngprague.cz; Tue–Sun 10am–6pm), or Trade Fair Palace, is one of the earliest large-scale Functionalist buildings in Europe. It was built by Oldřich Tyl and Josef Fuchs in 1929 to house exhibitions showcasing Czech industrial expertise. It was used for industrial exhibitions until 1951, then as the offices for foreign trade companies until 1974, when it was badly damaged in a fire. Rebuilt in 1995, it now houses the National Gallery's collections of 20th- and 21st-century art, and some of the holdings of 19th-century paintings and sculpture.

As part of a major reorganisation the National Gallery has moved its 19th-century Czech collection to Salm Palace (Salmovský palác; see page 33). This has freed up space for the work of 19th-, 20th- and 21st-century international artists, as well as more modern and contemporary Czech art.

On the left as you enter is a bookshop, and at the far end of the ground floor, near the stairs and lifts, is **Café**

'Tahitian idyll', by Paul Gauguin

Jedna, see ②. Begin the tour by taking the lift to the third floor.

Czech Art 1900–30

The first space in the galleries on the third floor is given over to the works of František Kupka (1871–1957), from his early Symbolist paintings such as *The Path of Silence I* (1903), to those in the Fauvist style, such as *Family Portrait* (1910), via the transitional *Two-Colour Fugue – Amorpha* (1912), to his later outright abstraction, as in *Vertical Planes III* (1912–13) and the De Stijl-like *Series CVI* (1935–6).

Next are the experimental photographic works of František Drtikol (1883–1961), with their Art Deco feel. Then there is the Cubism at which Czech artists so excelled. Look out for Emil Filla's *Salome* (1911–12) and the unsurpassed furniture and ceramics of Josef Gočar (1880–1945) and Pavel Janák (1882–1956). Another luminary of the Czech avant-garde, Bohumil Kubišta, seems – strangely given his name – more Futurist than Cubist (see *Meditation*, 1915). In contrast, the works of Gutfreund, Čapek and Špála seem less convincing and were dated by the time they were produced.

Other exhibits of particular interest in this section are those related more to design than high art. There are many fascinating works in the genres of book illustration, stage design, fashion, architecture, aircraft design and furniture. Look out in particular for the models, drawings and photographs of the architects Aldolf Loos and Ludvík Kysela.

French Art

The highlight of the museum for many people will be the galleries of French art, which are also on the third floor. Thanks to state acquisitions of major collections in 1923 and 1960, and numerous individual acquisitions in between, hardly any major French painter from the mid-19th to early 20th century is not represented here.

Displays begin with busts by Rodin, three small pictures by Delacroix and a couple of paintings by Corot. The gallery also contains fine works from Courbet, notably *Woman in a Straw Hat with Flowers* (1857) and *Forest Grotto* (c.1865).

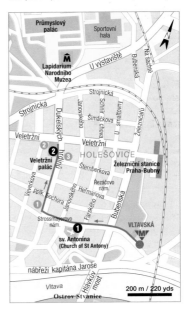

The Impressionists are particularly well represented, especially by Pissarro (*In the Kitchen Garden*, 1881), and *Garden at Val Hermeil*, 1880) and Sisley (*The Bridge at Sèvres, 1877*, and *Bourgogne Lock at Moret*, 1882). There are also a couple of early works by Monet: *Orchard Trees in Blossom* (1879) and *Women among Flowers* (1875). The academic side of Degas is visible in his *Portrait of Lorenzo Pagans* (1882), and there is a slightly sentimental picture by Renoir, *The Lovers* (1875).

Toulouse-Lautrec's picture of two women dancing together, *At the Moulin Rouge* (1892), is a fine example of the artist's output. There is also a strong showing of Gauguin's work – look out in particular for *Flight* (1902). Van Gogh is represented by the vibrant canvas *Green Wheat* (1889). Perhaps most impressive all, though, is the group of 19 works by Picasso, from the early *Seated Female Nude* (1906) to a wide range of his Cubist paintings.

The gallery has three outstanding works by Cézanne: *Portrait of Joachim Gasquet* (1896–7), *House in Aix-en-Provence* (1885–7) and *Fruits* (1879–82). There are also pictures by Rousseau, Seurat, Braque and Derain, including the latter's wonderful *Cadaquès* (1910) and *Montreuil-sur-Mer* (also 1910).

Also present are works by Despiau, Dufy, Chagall and Bourdelle. Matisse is represented by a series of his lithographs as well as by the intriguing *Joaquine* (1910). At the end of the collection, look out for Maillol's beautiful chalk drawing, *Female Nude* (1902).

Art from 1930 to the present day

The collections on the second floor begin with a welcome invitation to sit down in a little cinema in a side room. Here, there is a display celebrating the work of the master puppeteer and animator Jiří Trnka (1912–69), sometimes described as the 'Disney of the East'. There are also screenings of extracts from classic Czech films.

Czech artists made a distinctive contribution to Surrealism, and are represented in the succeeding galleries by Jindřich Štyrský (1899–1942), by the female artist who went under the name of Toyen (1902–80), and by the bizarre illuminated sculptures of Zdeněk Pešánek (1896–1965).

The grimness of the wartime Occupation is expressed in works by the artists of Group 42. Works such as *Railroad Station* with a *Windmill* by František Hudeček (b.1909) combine the artistic innovations of the previous decades with a fascination with industry and technology.

The post-war landscape looked hardly less optimistic. After 1948, Socialist Realism was the only recognised artistic creed. Art became divided into the official and unofficial, and any artists deemed to be either 'individualists' or 'formalists' were driven underground. The situation is well illustrated in the next few sections of the gallery. There is a small display of Socialist-Realist paintings (most of the gallery's holdings of art of this type languish in disgrace in store). Then there are much larger spaces devoted to art-

ists who worked outside the official ideology. One area where, exceptionally, the official channels for creativity did engender some inspiration was that of industrial and domestic design: a display of items sent to the Brussels Expo of 1958 – including glass, ceramics and furniture – shows work at the forefront of its field.

20th- and 21st-century Foreign Art

On the first floor is the collection of Foreign Art, which has particular strength and depth in Austrian and German Expressionist art. Among the finest examples from this movement are *Operation* (1912) by Max Oppenheimer, *Pregnant Woman and Death* (1911) by Egon Schiele, and *Portrait of the Poet Albert Ehrenstein* (1913–14) by Oskar Kokoschka. Kokoschka's townscapes of Prague painted in 1934–5 are also displayed nearby. In this context, look out too for the earlier, proto-Expressionist works by Edvard Munch: *Dancing on a Shore* (1900) and *Seashore Landscape near Lübeck* (1907).

Moving on, there are two fine Secessionist works by Gustav Klimt – *Virgin* (1913) and *Castle with Moat* (1908–9) – and two large Cubist-inspired paintings by Aristarkh Lentulov: *A Ballet Theme* (1912) and *Landscape near Kislovodsk* (1913). Meanwhile, Paul Klee's mesmerising *Tropical Forest* (1915) is difficult to fit into any established art-historical category.

Thereafter, the collection is patchy in its continuation of the story of 20th-century art, although there are pieces by Miró and Picasso, Henry Moore, Joseph Beuys and Antoni Tàpies. And even if the quality of the collection is uneven, it sharpens the impression the few masterpieces make to have them displayed next to less-inspired works.

When you have finished, repair to the pub across the road from the museum, **Restaurace U Houbaře**, for refreshments, see ❸.

Food and Drink

❶ LIBERŠKÉ LAHŮDKY

Dukelských hrdinů 33; tel: 739 047 959; Mon–Fri 7am–7pm, Sat–Sun 8am–6pm; €
A branch of a small chain of dependable delicatessens. Serves sandwiches, filled rolls, cooked meats, schnitzels, salads and excellent cakes and pastries. Very inexpensive.

❷ CAFÉ JEDNA

Veletržní palác; opening times as for museum; €
This restaurant is cheap, egalitarian and basic. It serves sandwiches, soups and other unreconstructed Communist rations. The daily hot dish is sustaining, if redolent of school dinners.

❸ RESTAURACE U HOUBAŘE

Dukelských hrdinů 30; tel: 720 625 923; daily 11am–midnight; €
Straightforward pub, serving simple Czech food – fried cheese, pork steaks, dumplings – and Pilsner Urquell to a regular crowd.

Průmyslový Palace and the Lapidarium

VÝSTAVIŠTĚ TO TROJA

This full-day tour involves a visit to a huge Art Nouveau exhibition hall and a stroll through Stromovka Park and across the river to a Baroque château, before ending up in Prague's botanical gardens.

DISTANCE: 4km (2.5 miles)
TIME: A full day
START: Průmyslový Palace
END: Prague Botanical Garden
POINTS TO NOTE: Note that this tour visits the area just to the north of the one covered in route 12, so an option might be to combine the two, albeit by flitting past some sights to fit everything in. There are very few decent cafés and restaurants on the way to Troja; in summer there is a café in the palace grounds, a café outside the zoo (many more options inside) and a tea stall in the botanical garden. A good option is to take food and drink with you, as the Stromovka park is a great place for a picnic. It's also a lovely place for children to run around in, which, coupled with a trip to the zoo, makes this a good route to do with kids.

The northern reaches of the city are often ignored by tourists, but contain important sights, including one of Prague's first Art Nouveau buildings, a fine Baroque palace, a zoo and the city's Botanical Garden.

VÝSTAVIŠTĚ EXHIBITION GROUND

Dominating the view down the long street of Dukelských hrdinů is the huge and ornate **Průmyslový Palace** ❶ (Průmyslový palác), part of the Výstaviště Exhibition Ground. Designed by František Prášil and Bedřich Münzberger, it was constructed for the Exhibition of 1891. One of the very first Art Nouveau buildings in Prague, it is still used for trade fairs and exhibitions – which vary hugely, from the mundane to the erotic – but when there is no show on it can appear a little strange and bleak.

To the rear of the main exhibition hall is the Křižík Fountain, designed by the electrical pioneer František Křižík. A masterpiece of kitsch, the fountain comprises hundreds of individually controlled jets and lights, all set to music.

The Troja Château and its formal gardens

The Lapidarium

To the right of the Průmyslový Palace, in one of the side pavilions, is the National Museum's **Lapidarium** ❷ (www.nm.cz; May–Nov Wed 10am–4pm, Thu–Sun noon–6pm). This contains a collection of Bohemian stone sculptures from the 11th to 19th centuries, many of which at one time adorned the city. As well as information on the mining, selection and preparation of rocks used for stone carving, this chronologically arranged exhibition includes some outstanding works of art. Among the Romanesque and Gothic exhibits, one of the finest is the original of the bronze equestrian statue of St George, which originally stood outside St Vitus (now replaced by a copy). Also here is the original tympanum from the Týn Church (1380–90) and Petr Parléř's exceptional figures from the Old Town Bridge Tower, as well as the original pillar and statue of the Bruncvík.

The Renaissance exhibits are dominated by the Krocín fountain that used to stand in Staroměstské náměstí. And the Baroque pieces include the original (earlier) equestrian statue of St Wenceslas from Wenceslas Square, as well as a series of interesting gilded and brightly painted statues.

The remainder of the collection is given over to works from the 19th century. Notable among these are the two tombs made by Václav Prachner and the four allegorical groups designed for the cupola of the National Museum by Bohuslav Schnirch.

Behind the Lapidarium is **Sea World** (Mořský Svět; www.morsky-svet.cz; Mon–Fri 8.30am–6pm, Sat–Sun 9am–7pm), a small aquarium that features sharks.

The Panorama

Also in the grounds of Výstaviště, behind the main exhibition hall, is the newly restored **Panorama** ❸ (Apr–Oct Tue–Fri 1–5pm, Sat–Sun 10am–5pm). Panoramas were very popular during the 19th century – especially of subjects that portrayed patriotic themes – and this huge circular painting by Luděk Marold (1865–98) depicts The Battle of Lipany of 1434, when citizens of Prague helped defeat the Hussite army of Prokop Holý.

Prague Zoo resident

STROMOVKA PARK

To the left of the main entrance to Výstaviště is the way into **Stromovka ❹**. Previously a royal hunting ground, this wooded park became a public space at the beginning of the 19th century and is one of the most extensive open spaces in the city. A signposted foot- and cycle-path leads through the park towards the Troja château. A turn-off to the right takes you under the railway line and over a footbridge to Císařský ostrov (Emperor's Island). The path continues straight across the island to an elegant modern footbridge. On the other side turn left along the river and then right onto on U trojského zámku.

TROJA CHÂTEAU

Here is the entrance to the **Troja Château ❺** (Trojský zámek; www.ghmp. cz; Tue–Sun 10am–6pm, Fri 1–6pm; the Trojská karta joint ticket gives you access to the château, zoo and botanical garden). The building is set in large formal gardens (open until 7pm), part of which are given over to a large apple orchard.

Built in 1685 by Jean-Baptiste Mathey for Václav Vojtěch of Sternberg, this large Baroque mansion has an ornate interior covered in frescoes on Classical themes (not greatly enhanced by a bodged restoration). The château and gardens suffered greatly in the 2002 floods, but much of the damage has now

been repaired. Approaching through the gardens does give you a view of the southern facade, with its staircase decorated by monumental sculpture representing the battle between the gods and Titans.

The interior

When you enter the building, you will be given a pair of overshoes, designed to protect the floors. The château is home to a collection of 19th-century Czech painting, the highlights of which are probably the landscapes on display in the first few rooms. Many of the same artists are represented as in the National Gallery's collection of 19th-century art; of particular interest are Ludvík Kohl's highly Romantic *Gothic Hall with a Meeting of a Secret Brotherhood* (1812); two lovely landscapes of mountain waterfalls by Charlotta Peipenhagenová (1880s); *Forest Scene* (1853) by Josef Mánes; and the virtuoso *Path in a Deciduous Forest* by Bedřich Havránek (1878).

The rooms upstairs are particularly wonderfully decorated, especially the Grand Hall, which is covered in frescoes by Abraham Godyn (1663–1724).

PRAGUE ZOO

Just outside the Troja Château is the stop for the No. 112 bus, behind which is the entrance to **Prague Zoo ❻** (Zoologická zahrada; U Trojského zámku 3; www. zoopraha.cz; daily June–Aug

Troja Château

Autumn hues in Stromovka park

9am–9pm, Apr–May and Sept–Oct 9am–6pm, Mar 9am–5pm, Nov–Feb 9am–4pm). Spacious and well-kept enclosures are home to around 650 species. Extensive grounds stretch out over a lush river valley up a steep, rocky escarpment to rolling meadows. Animals range from penguins, big cats and elephants to giraffes, hippos and polar bears, which can be viewed via glass-fronted indoor viewing platforms and walkways if they are outdoors. The zoo was particularly badly affected by the 2002 flood, when there were tragic scenes of the animals trying to cope with the rising waters.

PRAGUE BOTANICAL GARDEN

From the zoo, head further uphill, taking the footpath that leads off right from the road that climbs the hill above the château. A sign points you towards the Botanická zahrada Praha. At the top turn left to the main entrance to **Prague Botanical Garden** ❼ (Botanická zahrada Praha; www.botanicka.cz; daily May–Sept 9am–7pm, Apr 9am–6pm, Oct and Mar 9am–5pm, Nov–Feb 9am–4pm).

The gardens are very extensive and include, among other things, a Mediterranean and Japanese garden, medicinal and poisonous plants, as well as a perennial flower bed. Also attached to the garden, cascading down the hill towards the château, is the St Clara vineyard Established during the reign of King Václav II in the 13th century, today it is partly maintained for its heritage value, and partly as a fully working wine-producing business. The historic collection of vines includes an almost complete set of the approximately 50 grape varieties that are officially cultivated in Bohemia. In addition to an exhibition on viticulture, a selection of wines is for sale at the old vineyard house. The view from the top of the hill by the St Clara chapel is lovely.

Fata Morgana

Following the road up to the right of the main entrance brings you to the curving **Fata Morgana Glasshouse** ❽ (Skleník Fata Morgana; Tue–Sun, same times as the gardens). Divided into three main sections – semi-desert, tropical rainforest and cloud forest – it is now well established and the plants are flourishing. From the dry zone a subterranean passage leads through a divided pool, one side for the Americas, the other for Africa and Asia, before emerging into the hot and steamy tropics – very green, with huge tropical butterflies flitting amongst the plants. However, perhaps even more interesting is the cooler cloud-forest room, where jets provide a constant mist of water. Above, the glasshouse footpaths lead through an attractive woodland with picnic and play areas.

To get back into town, return to the bus stop outside the zoo entrance and take the No. 112 to Nádraží Holešovice metro station.

Staropramen Brewery

SMÍCHOV

Once a country district popular with aristocrats for their summer retreats, then, in the 19th century, an industrial working-class enclave, today Smíchov is noted as the location of the Staropramen Brewery and the Ethnographical Museum in the gorgeous Villa Kinský.

DISTANCE: 2km (1.25 miles)
TIME: A half day
START: Anděl metro station
END: Ethnographical Museum
POINTS TO NOTE: Staropramen Brewery is open every day but best to book ahead for tours.

The route begins on your arrival at **Anděl metro station ❶**. This station was built as a Communist showpiece and used to be known as Moskevská (Moscow) – a gesture of friendship towards the Soviet Union, and a point hammered home with a number of large murals showing triumphant workers striding into the future. Opposite the platforms, you can still see today eight bronze reliefs, one showing two cosmonauts, another with a young girl waving flags marked 'Moskva' and 'Praha'.

Ascending the escalators, you emerge in the Nový Smíchov Shopping Centre, a showpiece of the new capitalist Prague and the city's largest, flashiest mall. The name 'Anděl' means 'angel', and so the centre's architect, Jean Nouvel, has had a 21st-century angel depicted on the glass facade, along with quotations (in red) from Czech literature, including from the works of Franz Kafka.

STAROPRAMEN BREWERY

As you exit the building, make your way south, down Nádražní to the enormous **Staropramen Brewery ❷** (Pivovary Staropramen; www.staropramen.com) at No. 84. Attached to the brewery is a pub and restaurant, **Potrefená Husa Na Verandách**, see ❶, serving, of course, extremely good beer. It is also possible to see the inside the brewery on a guided tour starting in the visitor centre (entrance via the doorway on Pivovarská on the east side; daily 10am–6pm). There are generally tours in English at 10am and 1pm, and usually one at 4pm as well. Check the website for details and to book.

The tour

The 50-minute tours begin with a short film outlining Staropramen's history

<table>
</table>

Anděl station bronze   *A refreshing beer at the end of the brewery tour*

from its construction in 1869 to its present operations as part of a multi-national company. Visitors then proceed to Brewhouse No. 1, where the first stages in beer production are demonstrated, followed by Brewhouse No. 5, which exhibits the fermentation and ageing processes, filtration, bottling and quality control, and finally there is a visit to the New Brewhouse. The tour ends with a beer-tasting session. If after that, however, you are still thirsty (or perhaps hungry), walk back up along Nádražní and just before the crossroads and the metro station try the Mexican restaurant at No. 21 on the left, **Hombre del Mundo**, see ➋.

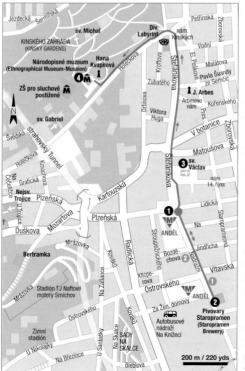

STEFÁNIKOVA

Walking north again, continue over the crossroads past the metro station on to Stefánikova. Soon, on your right, is the barn-like **Church of St Václav** ➌, built in 1885 to designs by Antonín Barvitius. Behind it is the small park of náměstí 14 října, while on the northern side of the square, beside the church, is the **Portheimka**, a small 18th-century mansion built by Kilián Ignáz Dientzenhofer (one of the architects of St Nicholas's Church in nearby Malá Strana) as his town residence.

VILLA KINSKY

Now walk (or take bus 58 or 59) up Stefánikova to the southeast corner of

Villa Kinsky in the snow

the Kinský Gardens (south of Petřín Hill) and turn left on to Holečkova. A 10-minute walk then brings you to the gorgeous empire-style **Villa Kinský** on your right – now the **Ethnographical Museum-Musaion ❹** (Kinského zahrada 98; www.nm.cz; Tue–Sun 10am–6pm). This houses the folk collection of the National Museum, with high-quality displays on traditional Czech art, music,

costume, farming methods and handicrafts. Three artisans' workshops have been recreated as part of the exhibition, and demonstrations of crafts such as blacksmithing and woodcarving are frequently held. There are also regular folk concerts and temporary exhibitions covering topics from banditry to terriculology (the science of scarecrows).

The **Kinský Gardens** are the perfect place for a stroll on a sunny day. Created by Count Rudolf Kinský in 1825 they were developed in celebration of the Czech National Revival to create a natural landscape to honour the Czech countryside.

Bertramka Villa

To the west of Anděl metro station (up Plžeňská, Kartouzská and then the leafy lane of Mozartova) is the Bertramka Villa, once the Mozart Museum. In the 18th century, this fine vineyard manor house was the country villa of František Dušek and his young wife, the singer Josefina Dušková. It was here that Mozart stayed on his visits to Prague in 1787 and 1791, and here that he composed the aria 'Bella mia fiamma, addio' from *Don Giovanni* for Josefina. He also, allegedly, scrawled out the overture to the opera the night before its première at the Estates Theatre (see page 118) in the city centre. Sadly, the museum closed in 2009 after a protracted restitution case ended with the apparently disgruntled previous tenant and manager of the museum stripping the place bare and now it is in poor state of repair. The rightful owners, the Czech Mozart Society are trying to raise funds to renovate and reopen the museum.

Food and Drink

❶ POTREFENÁ HUSA NA VERANDÁCH

Nádražní 84; tel: 257 191 200; www.phnaverandach.cz; daily 11am–midnight (until 1am Thu–Sat); €
Smart, modern bar-restaurant offering a large selection of beer alongside traditional high-carb Czech food to soak up the alcohol. Good value.

❷ HOMBRE DEL MUNDO

Nádražní 21; tel: 257 326 902; www.hombredelmundo.cz; daily 11am–midnight; €
For a complete change from Czech fare, try this Mexican alternative. Choose from tacos, fajitas, enchiladas and burritos or grilled meats, salads and desserts such as churros.

Vintage trams at the Transport Museum

TRANSPORT MUSEUM AND MÜLLER VILLA

Although this route has to be planned in advance, it is well worth thinking ahead, as the arch-Modernist Müller Villa is one of the least-known but most rewarding sights in all of Prague.

DISTANCE: 1km (0.75 mile)
TIME: A half day
START: Public Transport Museum
END: Müller Villa
POINTS TO NOTE: There is nowhere to eat en route, but this tour is relatively short and the tram service quick and frequent, so it is recommended to eat in town before you set off, or after the visit has finished. Note that the Transport Museum is only open at weekends, while the Müller Villa is also open on Tuesday and Thursday but must be booked in advance.

This route may be short, but it includes one of the Prague's most worthwhile sights for anyone interested in the history of art and design. First, a transport museum gives an overview of how the city's exemplary public transport system developed over the past 100 years or more, while the latter half of the route takes you around a gem of Modernist design.

TRANSPORT MUSEUM

Begin at the Vozovna Střešovice tram stop (tram Nos 1, 2, and 22 will bring you here). This is just outside the **Public Transport Museum ❶** (Muzeum městské hromadné dopravy; www.dpp.cz; Apr–mid-Nov Sat–Sun 9am–5pm). Set in an old tram shed, this is also where the 'nostalgic' tram No. 91 begins and ends its journey (see www.dpp.cz for times).

The collection

The museum's collection of trams and trolley buses outlines the history of public transport in the city, from a horse-drawn tram dating from 1886 to a bus dating from 1985. Some of the early trams are beautifully made and decorated in Art Nouveau style, and there is a good exhibition showing the building of the city's metro system.

MÜLLER VILLA

Just around the corner, at Nad hradním vodojemem 14, is the **Müller Villa ❷**

The Müller Villa

(Müllerova vila; www.mullerovavila.cz; admission only on guided tours that must be booked in advance, Tue, Thu, Sat–Sun Apr–Oct 9am, 11am, 1pm, 3pm and 5pm, Nov–Mar 10am, noon, 2pm and 4pm), Prague's only example of the work of architect Adolf Loos (see box). The villa was designed and built in 1930 for the wealthy construction magnate František Müller and his wife Milada. As befits an iconic Modernist building, the exterior is plain and severe, but the beautifully designed interiors are luxurious.

The tour, limited to around seven people at a time, is very informative and lasts around an hour. It takes you around all the public and private areas of the villa. Even the heating system and utility rooms show just how well-integrated Loos' design was.

Now that the villa has been restored to its former glory, visitors can fully appreciate the building's layout and the use of colour as an element in the organisation of the overall design. Particularly appealing elements are the open-plan living room with its large windows and dining space above, the 'boudoir', a cosy space that acted as a private retreat, and the elegant lady's dressing room – no doubt a favourite of Mrs Müller.

Adolf Loos

One of the most important architects of early Modernism, Adolf Loos was born in Brno in 1870, then part of the Austro-Hungarian Empire. He trained in Vienna and, after a short period in North America, soon established a reputation as an iconoclast, particularly following the publication of his most influential work, *Ornament and Crime*, in 1908. This outlined his ideas on decoration (he repudiated it), and these were put into effect in one of his most important buildings, the Michaeler House (1911) in Vienna. The blank, featureless facade was revolutionary and even raised the ire of the emperor, who had to look out on it from the Hofburg. Loos developed this ethos further in his designs for domestic buildings, notably the Steiner House (Vienna, 1910) and the Müller Villa in Prague. He died near Vienna in 1933.

All the way up Karlštejn Castle

KARLŠTEJN

If you're feeling a little claustrophobic in Prague, make an excursion, by train or car, to Karlštejn Castle. Traipse round the castle, picnic by the river, drink a beer in a pub, and then have a snooze on the journey home.

DISTANCE: 60km (38 miles) rtn
TIME: A half day
START: Prague
END: Karlštejn Castle
POINTS TO NOTE: Trains from Prague leave the main railway station (Hlavní nádraží) every hour from about 8am (journey time around 45 minutes). Alternatively, take metro line B to Smíchovské nádraží, and catch a train there. By road, take the E50–D5 (Route 5) towards Plzeà, leave the motorway at exit 10 (at Lodúnice) and follow the signs to Karlštejn. Note that Karlštejn Castle's Tour 2 needs to be pre-booked.

Some 30km (19 miles) southwest of Prague, in a romantic forested setting, is **Karlštejn Castle** (www.hradkarlstejn.cz; July–Aug daily 9am–6.30pm, Tue–Sun, May, June and Sept 9.30am–5.30pm, Mar–Apr Mar–Apr 9.30am–4pm, Oct 9.30am–4.30pm, Nov–Dec Sat–Sun 10am–3pm, closed noon–1pm all year).

The castle was built in 1365, possibly under the direction of Matthew of Arras,

first architect of St Vitus's Cathedral in Prague; it was modified during Renaissance times then fell into near decay. Magnificent as it is, much of what we see today is a zealous late 19th-century reconstruction by conservation architect Josef Mocker, who attempted to return the castle to its original Gothic appearance.

REACHING THE CASTLE

If you arrive by train, it is a 10-minute walk from **Karlštejn station** across the bridge to the village. From there, continue along the main street to make the steep ascent to the castle (a further 15-minute walk).

Those arriving in Karlštejn at midday may wish to lunch at **Taverna U ezopa**, see ❶. Alternatively, bring a picnic to eat on the banks of the Berounka River, or stop at one of the grocery shops in the village. In peak season it may be best to arrive early in the morning, before the coach parties arrive.

Castle walls

As you approach **Karlštejn Castle** (Hrad Karlštejn), you can appreciate the massive walls and protruding cliffs that made it

The castle's seemingly impenetrable towers

impregnable over the centuries. However, Emperor Charles IV, for whom Karlštejn was built, did not intend it to be a military stronghold; strategically speaking it would have served no useful purpose. He had it built solely to safeguard the holy relics and coronation insignia of the kingdom.

Holy relics

During medieval times the holy relics housed within the castle were of huge significance: they included what are said to be two thorns from Jesus's crown, a fragment of the sponge soaked in vinegar and offered to him on the cross, one of St John the Baptist's teeth and the arm of St Anne. To possess such treasures was seen as a sign of God's favour, a blessing for the emperor and his subjects. The collection of

relics was presented twice a year for public worship: on the Friday after Easter, the Day of the Holy Relics, and on 29 November, the anniversary of Charles IV's death. Mass is still celebrated in the Chapel of the Cross, where the precious items are kept.

CASTLE INTERIOR

Inside, visitors must join one of three guided tours (available in several languages).

Tour 1

This tour explores the interiors of the Imperial Palace and the lower floors of the Marian Tower. These include the Knights' Hall, the Audience Chamber and the private apartments of the emperor and his wife, which are decorated with furnishings from

Medieval walls

the 14th to the 19th century. Then there is the Treasury and Jewel Hall, where you can see treasures from the Chapel of the Holy Cross, as well as a replica of St Wenceslas's Crown. You can also see the former castle prison. The tour lasts about an hour.

Tour 2

This tour lasts about 1 hour 40 minutes and is only available from May to October. It is the only tour which needs to be booked in advance (tel: 311 681 617) – worth the effort since it gives you access to one of the most illustrious medieval sanctuaries on the continent, the Chapel of the Holy Cross.

The tour also takes in the Marian and Great towers before heading to the heavily ornamented library. Next is the Church of Our Lady then the Chapel of St Catherine, adorned with semi-precious stones. This is where Charles IV spent time in meditation – his portrait, with his second wife Anna von Schwednitz, is above the doorway.

Finest of all, though, is the **Chapel of the Holy Cross**. It is divided into two sections by a golden railing; the precious relics were preserved in the sanctuary, which only the emperor and the priests were allowed to enter. The gold walls and ceilings of the chapel are studded with more than 2,000 semi-precious stones (note also the 32 Venetian-glass stars embedded in the ceiling). The walls also feature 129 painted panels executed by Master Theodoric in the 1360s.

Tour 3

A third tour also lasts about 1 hour 40 minutes and is available only from May to November. The tour is similar to Tour 2, but includes the third, fourth and fifth floors of the Great Tower and misses out the Chapel of the Holy Cross.

Zbraslav

Also south of Prague is the pretty town of Zbraslav, 12km (7 miles) along the River Vltava. It was once popular with day-trippers from Prague who swarmed off the paddle steamers (see www.paroplavba.cz for the modern equivalent) to be entertained by the brass bands playing in pubs and riverside cafés. One of the most prolific Czech composers of waltzes and polkas for brass bands came from Zbraslav – Jaromir Vejvoda. His tune, 'koda lásky' ('What a Shame about Love') was one of the great hits of the mid-20th century, though it is better known abroad by its English or German titles ('Roll out the Barrel' or 'Rosamunde'). A restaurant on the town square is almost a shrine to Vejvoda.

Food and Drink

● TAVERNA U EZOPA
Karlštejn 200; tel: 311 572 380;
www.reckarestauraceezop.cz; Mon–Tue
1–9pm, Fri–Sun noon–10pm; €
This attractive rustic restaurant serves some excellent Greek dishes including stuffed peppers and lamb kleftiko.

DIRECTORY

Hand-picked hotels and restaurants to suit all budgets and tastes, organised by area, plus select nightlife listings, an alphabetical listing of practical information, a language guide and an overview of the best books and films to give you a flavour of the city.

Upmarket Alchymist Residence Nosticova

ACCOMMODATION

The choice of accommodation in Prague is vast, from fabulous historic palaces and uber-cool modern establishments to friendly family hotels and trendy hostels. Choosing a hotel can be daunting but it is worth taking some time to consider which areas appeal both to your criteria and your pocket.

Prague is a popular destination all-year round so it is always advisable to book well in advance. However outside the high summer season and the run up to Christmas, bargains can be found and prices fluctuate dramatically. Being a tram or metro ride outside the city centre can often mean you can get quality at a good price. Hostels too can be good value but they do get booked up well ahead. Room rates are usually quoted in euros and not in Czech crowns.

For those looking for a quieter option Mala Straná across the river may prove ideal. This historic castle district is hillier and has less public transport links but it is more laid back and perfect for a romantic break or family holiday. A walk across the Charles Bridge will bring you into Old Town. The Old Town or Staré Město attracts the most tourists and can be more expensive. It still retains its historic atmosphere and is well connected by public transport and convenient for principal attractions. The New Town or Nové Město just to the south is fun and lively, more commercial and generally cheaper. It has good transport links and is still in walking distance of the historic centre. For those happy to be outside the centre try and choose a hotel close to a metro station. You will experience a more authentic Prague in areas such as Hradčany, Dejvice, Smíchov, Vinohrady and Žižkov.

Hradčany (Castle District)

Hotel Hoffmeister

Pod bruskou 7; tel: 251 017 111; www.hoffmeister.cz; metro: Malostranská; €€€

Situated on the corner of Chotkova as it winds up past the castle, the Hoffmeister is in a convenient location. It's not as attractive as some Prague hotels from the outside, but the rooms and facilities – which include a spa and a restaurant – are luxurious. The prices are surprisingly reasonable compared to some other Prague five-stars.

> Price for a double room for one night with breakfast:
>
> €€€€ = over 250 euros
> €€€ = 180–250 euros
> €€ = 120–180 euros
> € = below 120 euros

The Alchymist's opulent lobby

Savoy

Keplerova 6; tel: 224 302 430; www.hotelsavoyprague.com; tram 22; €€€
Overlooking the spires of the castle district, this Art Nouveau hotel features elegant rooms and bathrooms decorated in marble and chrome. The Hradčany Restaurant offers first-class international and Czech cuisine. It's also well-located to visit the Mala Straná district and Petřin Hill.

U krále karla

Úvoz 4; tel: 257 531 211; www.ukralekarla.com; tram: 22; €€€
This Baroque building is in a quiet and convenient location at the top of the Castle District, looking out over Petřín Hill and the Strahov. The rooms lean a little more towards Central European baronial kitsch than some, but many people will love the stained-glass windows.

U raka

Černínská 10; tel: 220 511 100; www.hoteluraka.cz; tram: 22; €€
Set in one of the only wooden houses left in Prague, and dating back to the mid-18th century, this complex is now a lovely hotel. The spotless rooms are beautifully laid out, and there is a delightful garden for the use of guests. It's quiet and romantic.

Malá Strana

Alchymist Residence Nosticova

Nosticova 1; tel: 257 312 513; www.nosticova.com; tram: 12, 22; €€€
If you have the money, this would be a delightful place to stay. Set above the excellent San Carlo restaurant, the fairy-tale apartments are furnished in an outrageously grand style (one even has a grand piano), and all have an attached bathroom and kitchen. Large reductions for stays during low season.

Design Hotel Neruda

Nerudova 44; tel: 257 535 557; www.designhotelneruda.com; tram: 12, 22; €€
Located just a stone's throw from the castle, this building dates back to 1348, but you'd never know it with its classy minimalist modern interior. You pay for the location as much as anything, but the rooms are clean and comfortable, and there is the pleasant Prague Chocolate café-cum-bistro.

Dům u tří čápů

Tomášská 16; tel: 257 210 779; www.hotelthreestorks.cz; tram: 12, 22; €€€
This up-to-the-minute design hotel close to the Waldstein Palace is an excellent choice. Very chic, all clean lines and modern furniture, but without disturbing the original fabric of the historic building. The rooms are also central and quiet, and the café and restaurant are good places to while away a few hours.

The lovely terrace at the Mandarin Oriental

Dům u velké boty

Vlašská 30; tel: 257 532 088;
www.dumuvelkeboty.cz; tram: 12, 22; €€
Opposite the German Embassy, this building dates from the early 17th century, and care has been taken to ensure that the interior and furniture maintain the historic feel. Comfortable beds, spotless bathrooms and friendly owners make it one of the best places to stay in the city. Cash only.

Hotel Aria

Tržiště 9; tel: 225 334 111; www.ariahotel.net; tram: 12, 22; €€€€
Expensive and heavy on designer chic, the Aria plays heavily on its musical theme. From Mozart to Dizzy Gillespie, each floor and room is dedicated to a particular music or musician. The fittings and fixtures are smart, and there's an in-house music library.

Mandarin Oriental

Nebovidská 1; tel: 233 088 888;
www.mandarinoriental.com/prague; tram: 12, 22; €€€€
Cleverly inserted into the fabric of a 14th-century monastery, this luxury establishment offers superlative comfort in a historic setting. Individually designed bedrooms, stylish public spaces, and a spa offering a sophisticated range of treatments.

Staré Město

Buddha-Bar Prague

Jakubská 8; tel: 221 776 300;
www.buddhabarhotelprague.com; metro: náměstí Republiky; €€€
If you are looking for something a bit different, the Buddha-Bar boutique hotel may be for you. Perfectly located near Old Town Square it's seductive, hip and sumptuous with low-lit rooms of red and gold. Live DJ in the slick Siddharta Café and there is also an Asian-themed spa.

Four Seasons Hotel

Veleslavínova 2a; tel: 221 427 000;
www.fourseasons.com/prague; metro: Staroměstská; €€€€
As well as an unsurpassable location close to Charles Bridge and with views over the Vltava to Malá Strana and the castle, the Four Seasons offers all the comfort and style associated with its name. A bonus is the CottoCrudo restaurant, a modern Italian, restaurant bar and lounge.

Grand Hotel Praha

Staroměstské náměstí 22; tel: 221 632 556; www.grandhotelpraha.cz; metro: Staroměstská; €€
This beautiful hotel occupies three historical buildings on Old Town Square. Rooms have wooden beams and immaculate period furniture. It may be a little of the noisy side, but it has a great view of the Astronomical Clock, especially from the baroque Café Mozart on the first floor.

Hotel Caruso

U Milosrdných 2; tel: 221 316 909;

Room at the Four Seasons

www.hotelcarusoprague.cz; metro: Staroměstská; €€
Located in Josefov, just a few minutes' walk from Old Town Square, this smart hotel boasts traditional features with modern furnishings. It combines comfort, convenience and very reasonable prices.

Hotel Century

Na Poříčí 7; tel: 221 800 800; www.sofitel. com; metro: náměstí Republiky; €€
This historic hotel offers very good value considering its high quality and excellent location just a stone's throw from Old Town Square, with metro and trams stops close by. The interior exudes contemporary elegance and facilities include an outside terrace for breakfast.

Hotel Černý slon

Týnská 1; tel: 222 321 521; www.hotelcernyslon.cz; metro: náměstí Republiky; €€
A lovely 14th-century building on the Unesco protected list, very close to Old Town Square. The rooms have been simply but attractively decorated with those in the attic featuring exposed beams.

Hotel Josef

Rybná 20; tel: 221 700 111; www.hoteljosef.com; metro: náměstí Republiky; €€€
A sleek designer hotel located near the Jewish Quarter. The interior, designed by Eva Jiřičná, has stone-and-glass bathrooms attached to minimalist rooms.

It certainly makes a change from the often heritage-heavy accommodation available elsewhere in the city.

Hotel Leonardo

Karoliny Světlé; tel: 239 009 239; www.hotelleonardo.cz; metro: Staroměstská; €€€
Just a few steps away from Charles Bridge but in a quiet side street, this boutique hotel offers charming accommodation decorated in the Art Nouveau style. The Platina Restaurant showcases modern Czech cuisine in a lovely courtyard garden setting.

Ventana Hotel

Celetna 7; tel: 221 776 600; www.ventana-hotel.net; metro: náměstí Republiky; €€€

The spa at the Mandarin Oriental

The glass-and-steel Anděl's

If you're looking for a change from the fake-baronial kitsch of many of Prague's top-end hotels, the Ventana presents a welcome respite. The decor is luxurious yet understated, modern yet comfortable, and the contemporary styling fits effortlessly with the historic fabric of the building.

Nové Město

987 Prague

Senovázné náměstí 15; tel: 255 737 200; www.987hotels.com; metro: náměstí Republiky; €€€

In the north of the New Town is this über chic design hotel. With Philippe Starck fixtures and Aera Saarinena and Arne Jacobsen furniture, it epitomises a certain kind of northern European cool design.

Adria

Václavské náměstí 26; tel: 221 081 111; www.adria.cz; metro: Mestek; €€

This bright, yellow-hued hotel is in an enviable position on Wenceslas Square and features rooms with polished wood furniture and green-gold fixtures. Adria has won awards for its green credentials and its Triton restaurant champions local producers.

Art Nouveau Palace Hotel

Panská 12; tel: 224 093 111; www.palace hotel.cz; metro: Mestek; €€€

A Secessionist landmark, built in 1909 as a luxury hotel. It still performs this function today, though now it is only the facade that retains an Art Nouveau appearance. The interior was gutted in the 1980s to make way for comfortable, if a little impersonal, modern rooms. However, this act of vandalism is offset by the luxury and excellent service.

Boscolo Prague

Senovázné náměstí 13; tel: 224 593 111; www.prague.boscolohotels.com; metro: náměstí Republiky; €€€€

A grand 19th-century building painstakingly converted into a luxury hotel. The interior designers have let their imaginations run riot, with sumptuous rooms, a chic restaurant and a fabulous spa and pool. It can also be fabulously expensive, but perhaps worth it for this very continental version of extravagant comfort.

Hotel Elite

Ostrovní 32; tel: 211 156 100; www.hotel-elite.cz; metro: Národní třida; €

Not many hotels in the New Town have a suite protected by the municipality, but the Elite does, on account of its 17th-century painted ceiling. The other rooms have also been tastefully preserved, with wooden floors, period furniture and an uncluttered feel. The recently renovated Elite Garden restaurant gives the opportunity to eat lunch in or out.

Hotel Yasmin

Politických vězňů 12; tel: 234 100 100; www.hotel-yasmin.cz; metro: Muzeum; €€

Just one block away from Wenceslas Square, this stunning designer estab-

Strong colours at the Angelo

lishment is linked to Prague's most famous thoroughfare by an arcade. The rooms and suites are furnished in shades of grey and green and the public spaces are adorned with unique sculptures. The chic noodle bar serves some excellent dishes from Italian to Thai.

Mosaic House

Odburo 4; tel: 221 595 350; www.mosaic house.com; metro: Karlova náměstí; €

This beautifully designed hostel has shared and private rooms, all with private bathrooms; the top floor ones have terraces with views over the city. Guests are invited to party at the La Loca Music Bar and Lounge.

Museum Pension

Mezibranská 15; tel: 296 325 186; www.hotelmuseum.cz; metro: Muzeum; €

Museum is a fantastic pension in a very central location next to the National Museum. The rooms are very large and all face a quiet courtyard garden. Perfect for families, the pension is excellent value for money and boasts a great buffet breakfast.

Further Afield

Anděl's

Stroupežnického 21, Prague 5; tel: 296 889 688; www.viennahouse.com/en/andels-prague; metro: Anděl; €€€

Although this glass-and-steel hotel may seem a little corporate at first, it has nice designer touches, elegant rooms and a luxurious feel. The hotel is flanked by a shopping mall and various eateries. There is also a restaurant and health club. Andel's is just 10 minutes away from the centre by metro.

Angelo

Radlická 1, Prague 5; tel: 234 801 111; www.viennahouse.com/en/angelo-prague; metro: Anděl; €€€

From the same stable as Andel's, Vienna House, this designer hotel is a good place to stay outside the city centre. Rooms feature strong colours and an Asian theme. Be sure to check out the restaurant and the stylish Jazz Bar.

Hotel Absolutum

Jablonského 4; tel: 222 541 406; www.absolutumhotel.cz; metro: Nádraží Holešovice; €€

Located in Holešovice, near the Výstaviště Exhibition Ground (see page 88) this boutique hotel combines chic contemporary styling with modern comforts such as a spa and wellness centre and a smart restaurant.

Hotel Adalbert

Břevnovský kláster, Markétská 1, Břevnov; tel: 220 406 170; www.hoteladalbert.cz; tram: 22, 57; €

This hotel is in an excellent and beautifully quiet location inside the Břevnov Monastery; convenient for both the city centre (by tram) and airport (by bus). The 18th-century building is very attractive and the comfortable rooms are excellent value.

RESTAURANTS

Prague's streets are chock-a-block with places to eat and the quality is improving all the time. Traditional Czech food, which is similar to other central European regional cuisines, still dominates among the increasing number of Thai, Italian, French and other world-cuisine options. There are a number of fast food chains as well, more so in the Nové Město area, such as McDonald's, KFC and Starbucks, plus the local equivalents.

In a city with such a wide choice of places to eat – and where many are of a similar quality making it difficult to decide – it is worthwhile selecting somewhere with a memorable setting. Enjoy a hearty meal beneath the vaults of a medieval cellar, dine in the stately surroundings of an historic palace, or sit at a table with stunning views over spires and the Vltava River.

Prague restaurants are attuned to the needs of visitors with young children, and many restaurants have non-smoking sections, provide highchairs and offer children's menus. Child-friendly establishments include Pizza Nuova, Pizzeria Grosseto and others, such as Taverna Olympos, which have seating outside.

Keep a watchful eye on the bill in Prague. Menu prices include value-added tax, but some waiters persist in adding it again to the total. In some of the more expensive restaurants, beware of the trays of *hors d'oeuvres* you may be offered; far from being complimentary, they may add substantially to the bill. Other items such as bread, butter, olives and mayonnaise also often cost extra.

Hradčany (Castle District)

U Císařů

Loretánská 5; tel: 220 518 484; www.ucisaru.cz; daily 10am–midnight; €€€
The hotel name translates as 'At the Emperor's'; appropriately, it is on the other side of the square from the Castle. The old-fashioned menu includes roast beef, pork knuckle and duck, and there are, surprisingly, a few vegetarian dishes.

Malá Strana

Aquarius

Tržiště 19; tel: 257 286 019; www.aquarius-prague.com; daily noon–3pm, 7pm–11pm; €€€€
Exquisitely decorated with Venetian stucco and hand-painted murals, this

The exquisite Aquarius

hotel restaurant is the place to come if you have done rather well out of the post-Communist privatisations. If you can afford to ignore the prices, the tasting menu and long wine list are of a high standard.

Café de Paris
Maltézské náměstí 4; tel: 603 160 718; www.cafedeparis.cz; daily 11.30am–midnight; €€
Set back in a delightful spot in Malá Strana, the accomplished French-inspired cuisine at this family-run establishment is matched by its excellent wine selection. No credit cards.

Coda
Tržiště 9; tel: 225 334 761; www.codarestaurant.cz; Mon–Sun 7am–11.30pm; €€€€
Set in the Aria Hotel this smart restaurant has a rooftop terrace offering spectacular views of the Lesser Town. It has a good tasting menu of Czech cuisine with traditional kulajda soup, roasted duck and plum ravioli, prepared by the Czech chef David Šašek.

El Centro
Maltézské náměstí 9; tel: 257 533 343; www.elcentro.cz; daily noon–midnight (closed Sat–Sun lunch); €€
Founded in 1999, El Centro was the first Spanish restaurant to set up in Prague. Authentic dishes from Andalucia and Latin America are served in a pleasant homey atmosphere. There is a selection of tasty tapas and the paella is renowned.

Lehka Hlava
Boršov 2/280; tel: 222 220 665; www.lehkahlava.cz; Mon–Fri 11.30am–11.30pm, Sat–Sun noon–11.30pm; €€
A short walk from Charles Bridge, the plain front of this vegetarian restaurant belies the eccentrically decorated interior. The menu incorporates influences from all over the world, including quesadillas, tofu red curry, tacos and kebabs.

Kampa Park
Na Kampě 8b; tel: 296 826 102; www.kampagroup.com; daily 11.30am–1am; €€€€
The food is good, and the views over the river are spectacular. The steep prices, however, may cause some indigestion. Popular with local celebrities.

Pálffy Palác
Valdštejnská 14; tel: 257 530 522; www.palffy.cz; daily 11am–11pm; €€€
Go through the door at the right-hand side of the imposing gateway and up the stairs to reach a dining hall that epitomises lavish faded glory: all gilded chandeliers and crystal. In operation since the 17th century, this restaurant has catered for everyone from diplomats to politicians in its time. An outdoor terrace leads out to breathtaking views of the castle. The European food is competent but unre-

Lunch with a view at Terasa U Zlate Studne

markable, but it is the surroundings that really count.

Terasa U Zlate Studne

U Zlaté studně 166/4; tel: 257 533 322; www.terasauzlatestudne.cz; daily 11am–11pm (Nov–Mar from noon); €€€€

On the roof of the Golden Well hotel, this elegant restaurant offers panoramic views of the Vltava and is ideal for a romantic dinner. The acclaimed chef Pavel Sapíc prepares a wonderful range of international dishes. There is a good list of international and Czech wines.

U Malířů

Maltézské náměstí 11; tel: 257 530 000; www.umaliru.cz; noon–11pm; €€€€

This restaurant is one the most expensive in Prague, found on a quiet square in the Lesser Quarter. French haute cuisine is served in a beautiful 15th-century dining room complete with an elaborately decorated ceiling, and a tiny outdoor terrace completes the picture. It's perfect for that special occasion.

U Modré kachničky

Nebovidská 6; tel: 257 320 308; www.umodrekachnicky.cz; daily noon–4pm, 6.30pm–midnight; €€€

This charming Bohemian restaurant serves fine duck and game dishes. Try fallow deer with rosehip sauce and Carlsbad dumplings or duck with walnut stuffing. Save space for the lovely fruit dumplings.

U Patrona

Dražického náměstí 4; tel: 257 530 725; www.upatrona.cz; daily 10am–midnight; €€€

These elegant little dining rooms close to the Charles Bridge at the Bridge Tower are a good place to try some well-prepared Czech specialities. The restaurant is set out over two floors, and you can sit outside on the romantic balcony for two.

Staré Město

Bakeshop Café and Bistro

Kozi 1, tel: 222 316 823; www.bakeshop.cz; daily 7am–9pm; €

Bakeshop has a wide variety of freshly made soups and sandwiches, plus interesting salads, and the selection of cakes are hard to resist. It's perfect for breakfast, lunch or a light evening meal.

Bellevue

Smetanovo nábřeží 18; tel: 222 221 443; www.bellevuerestaurant.cz; daily noon–3pm, 5.30–11pm; €€€€

Smart restaurant serving a competent version of modern international cuisine. Dishes such as roast veal loin with mushroom sauce are backed up by equally memorable desserts.

Brasileiro

U Radnice 8; tel: 224 234 474; www.ambi.cz; daily 11am–midnight; €€

One of the successful Ambiente group of restaurants, the Brasileiro specialises in

Choose CottoCrudo for contemporary Italian fare

Brazilian beef offered on an 'as-much-as-you-can-eat' basis. Accompany your meal with wine from Argentina.

Café Imperial

Na poříčí 15; tel: 246 011 440; www.cafeimperial.cz; daily 7am–11pm; €€

One of the grand old cafés of Prague, the Café Imperial is worth a visit just for the restored Art Nouveau interior with its wonderful tiling. Breakfast, lunch, afternoon tea and evening meals are served by friendly staff.

Café Montmartre

Retězová 7; tel: 222 221 244; Mon–Fri 9am–11pm, Sat–Sun noon–11pm; €

Historic café, once frequented by writers such as Jaroslav Hašek and Egon Erwin Kisch. Though no longer a hot-bed of political and cultural debate, it remains a pleasant place to sit, read and drink.

Café Slavia

Smetanovo nábřeži 2; www.cafeslavia.cz; tel: 224 218 493; daily 8am–midnight (Sat–Sun from 9am); €

This famous café, with views over the river and National Theatre, was once the haunt of artists and writers, including Václav Havel. The spacious and elegant Art Deco interior encourages you to linger, and morning coffee turns into lunch with a range of salads, pancakes and Czech dishes.

CottoCrudo

Four Seasons Hotel, Veleslavínova 2; tel: 221 426 880; www.cottocrudo.cz; daily 7am–11pm; €€€€

Replacing Allegro (the first Michelin-starred restaurant in post-Communist Eastern Europe), this sleek restaurant boasts Chef Luca de Astis, who adds a contemporary twist to authentic Italian dishes, beautifully cooked and presented using the best ingredients and artisan products from the Piedmont and Tuscany regions of Italy.

Kogo Havelská

Havelská 27; tel: 224 210 259; www.kogohavelska.cz; daily 11pm–11pm; €€

A relaxed but upmarket Italian restaurant located not far from Staroměstské náměstí. It offers the full range of Italian cuisine, with enticing starters and desserts. Booking is recommended.

Kolkovna Celnice

V celnice 4; tel: 224 212 240; www.kolkovna.cz; daily 11am–midnight; €€

Another Pilsner Urquell-owned beer hall, with all the advantages they bring of excellent beer and calorific Bohemian food. Celnice has the advantage of being on top of one of Prague's best clubs, where you can dance off the dumplings.

La Casa Argentina

Dlouhá 35; tel: 222 311 512;

The chandeliered Francouzscá, inside the Obecní dům building

www.lacasaargentina.cz; Tue–Sat
11:30am–2am; Sun–Mon 11.30am–1am;
€€€

The tastes and ambience of South
America have come to Prague at this
fun Argentinian restaurant serving the
best succulent steaks. Each room rep-
resents a different aspect of the country: a nautical tavern with lanterns and
swinging chairs; Buenos Aires piano
bar; and the Iguazu Falls.

La Dégustation

Haštalská 18; tel: 222 311 234;
www.ladegustation.cz; daily 6pm–midnight;
€€€

If you're feeling adventurous, this L-
shaped Michelin-star restaurant is one
of the finest in the city. Choose between
two tasting menus giving very different culinary experiences: the first (11
courses) is a gourmet ensemble carefully prepared by Chef Oldřich Saha-
jdák; the second offers a Bohemian
tasting selection (6 courses) that adds
a creative twist to traditional 19th- and
20th-century Czech cuisine.

Lokal

Dlouhá 33; tel: 222 316 265; www.ambi.cz;
Mon–Fri 11am–1am, Sun until midnight; €

Set on the edge of the Josefov district,
this friendly beer hall serves traditional,
home-made Czech fare made from
fresh ingredients and at reasonable
prices. You can also learn how to draw
beer form the bartenders, the courses
are held in Czech and English.

Maitrea

Týnská ulička 6; tel: 221 711 631;
www.restaurace-maitrea.cz; Mon–Fri
11.30am–11.30pm, Sat–Sun noon–11.30;
€

Over two floors, Maitrea is one of the
best meat-free options in Prague. The
feng-shui style creates a calm and
contemplative atmosphere with foun-
tains and Buddha statues adding to the
bespoke look.

Mlynec

Novotného lávka 9; tel: 227 000 777;
www.mlynec.cz; daily noon–3pm,
5.30–11pm; €€€

Mlynec is set in a beautiful location
by the river, with views of the Charles
Bridge. The degustation menu that can
feature dishes such as coquilles St-
Jacques, oxtail consommé and saddle
of deer is well worth trying.

Obecní dům

Náměstí Republiky 5; Francouzscá
restaurace: tel: 222 002 770;
www.francouzskarestaurace.cz; daily
noon–11pm; €€€€; Plzeňská restaurace: tel:
222 002 780; www.plzenskarestaurace.cz;
daily 11.30am–11pm; €€; Kavárna Obecní
dům; tel: 222 002 763; www.kavarnaod.cz;
daily 7.30am–11pm; €€

Prague's most opulent Art Nouveau
building is home to three eateries. The
finest, Francouzscá restaurace, is pricey
and French, offering passable food in
a spectacular gilded and chandeliered
interior. The café Kavárna Obecní dům

serves more basic meals and cakes in equally impressive surroundings. Downstairs in the basement is the cheaper, smartly decorated, Plzeňská restaurace, serving tasty Czech dishes in a beer hall atmosphere.

Pizza Nuova

Revoluční 1; tel: 221 803 308; http://pizzanuova.ambi.cz; daily 11am–11pm; €€

Tasty authentic Naples-style pizzas hand rolled and baked in a traditional oven using a beech wood fire. Pastas and meat dishes are also on the menu. Families dining here appreciate the kids' play room.

Pizzeria Rugantino

Dušní 4; tel: 222 318 172; www.rugantino. cz; Mon–Sat 11am–11pm, Sun noon–11pm; €€

Handily close to Old Town Square, the Rugantino serves large, tasty pizzas at reasonable prices. There is a no-smoking section at the front, overlooking the street, and the staff are friendly.

Potrefená husa

Platnéřská 9; tel: 224 813 819; www.potrefena-husa-praha.cz; Mon–Sat 11am–midnight, Sun noon–11pm; €€

Part of a successful chain, this lively, contemporary gastropub has a well-designed interior, moderate prices, updated Czech dishes and a good choice of drinks.

Le Terroir

Vejvodova 1; tel: 222 220 260; www.leterroir.cz; Tue–Sat 4–11pm; €€€

Set in vaulted brick cellars, Le Terroir boasts high-end, creative French-inspired cooking and an extensive wine cellar to complement the excellent food. The service is exceptional, too.

U medvídků

Na perštýně 7; tel: 224 211 916; www.umedvidku.cz; Mon–Sat 11.30am–11pm, Sun until 10pm; €€

This traditional beer hall, founded in 1466, is friendly, bustling and noisy. Excellent Budvar beer washes down a succession of classic Czech dishes, including hearty beef broth, pork with cabbage and dumplings and the ubiquitous fried cheese.

Ungelt

Týn 5; tel: 777 427 000; www.restaurant-ungelt.cz; daily 11am–midnight; €€€

In the charming surroundings of the cobbled Týn Court, behind the Týn Church, the restaurant offers a good variety of fish and meat dishes. An outdoor terrace makes a pretty setting for summertime dining. Specialities include lobster roasted in tarragon butter and rib-eye steak with roasted liver foie gras and black truffle poached in port wine.

U Vejvodů

Jilská 4; tel: 224 219 999; www.restauraceuvejvodu.cz; daily

9am–2am; €
From Gothic to Art Nouveau, the architectural styles provide an atmospheric Bohemian setting for traditional Czech and international cuisine, beer and live music.

La Veranda

Elišky Krásnohorské 2; tel: 224 814 733; www.laveranda.cz; Mon–Sat noon–11pm; €€€

A gourmet restaurant near the Spanish Synagogue, La Veranda is a light, stylish venue filled with flowers. It specialises in delicate fish dishes but has good meat and vegetarian options too. Cooking styles range from Mediterranean to pan-Asian. Excellent service and above average prices, but it's certainly worth the splurge.

Yami

Másna 3; tel: 222 312 756; www.yami.cz; daily noon–11pm; €€

Dine out on highly fresh Japanese and Korean dishes and succulent sushi at this small fusion restaurant. You can sit at the bar and watch the chefs prepare the food or relax at a table or outside in the garden.

Zlatá Praha

Intercontinental Hotel, Pařížská 30; tel: 296 630 914; www.zlatapraharestaurant.cz; Mon–Sat 6–11.30pm, Sun 11am–3pm; €€€

For an unforgettable dining experience, Zlatá Praha offers breathtaking views of the Old Town from the ninth floor of the Communist-era Intercontinental Hotel. Cutting-edge cooking consistently produces superb Czech and international dishes.

Nové Město

Alcron

Radisson SAS Alcron Hotel, Štěpánská 40; tel: 222 820 038; www.alcron.cz; Mon–Fri noon–2.30pm, 5.30–11.30pm, Sat 5.30–11.30pm; €€€€

Dating from the 1930s, the Radisson Hotel offers wonderful period decor as well as this decent fish restaurant. A varied menu, ranging from South-

The Art Deco Alcron

A view to dine for

East Asian to French dishes, uses fresh ingredients.

Café Louvre

Národní třída 22; tel: 224 930 949;
www.cafelouvre.cz; daily 8am–11.30pm
(Sat–Sun from 9pm); €

An elegant Art Nouveau café, much loved in the past by Prague's intellectuals, Café and Galerie Louvre is a great place to sit and browse through the papers. Below the café proper is a gallery displaying contemporary art, while upstairs you can get breakfast, lunch and an evening meal.

Cicala

Zitna 43; tel: 222 210 375;
www.trattoria.cz; Mon–Sat 11.30am–3pm,
5–10pm; €€

Set in a basement off a busy street, Cicala serves the most authentic, and some of the tastiest, Italian food in the city. The menu offers antipasti, pasta and meat dishes, plus daily specials.

Estella

Opatovická 17; tel: 777 431 344;
www.estrellarestaurant.cz; daily 11.30am–
10.30pm; €€

This excellent vegetarian restaurant serves tasty and inventive dishes, many cooked with organic ingredients. On offer are such classics as mushroom risotto or quinoa and spinach burgers. The Czech wines and beers are worth a try, as are the excellent teas and desserts. Cash only.

Globe Bookstore and Café

Pštrossova 6; tel: 224 934 203;
www.globebookstore.cz; Mon–Fri 10am–
midnight, Sat–Sun 9.30am–1am;
€

Well known as a centre of expat intellectual life. As well as the friendly café, with good coffee and light meals (pasta, salads and burgers), the book shop has occasional live music, lectures and book readings and signings. It is also one of the most pleasant, and cheapest, places to check your email.

Hybernia

Hybernská 7; tel: 222 226 004;
www.hybernia.cz; Mon–Fri 8am–midnight,
Sat–Sun 11am–midnight; €

Known for its generous portions and good value, this is a popular spot for reliable Czech fare not far from the Municipal House. There is an outside terrace for dining in warmer weather.

Kogo

Na Příkopě 22; tel: 221 451 259;
www.kogo.cz; daily 11am–11pm;
€€€

Kogo's a large, bustling, and very popular Mediterranean-style eatery in the contemporary Slovanský Dům arcade on Prague's main shopping street, which offers a vast range of fish, meat, and pasta dishes.

Lemon Leaf

Myslíkova 14; tel: 224 919 056;
www.lemon.cz; Mon–Fri 11am–11pm,

Sat–Sun noon–11pm (Sat until midnight);
€
This popular Nové Město eatery serves Thai favourites and other global dishes. Start with a refreshing papaya salad then try the green curry washed down with Czech beer.

Pivovarský dům

Ječná/Lípová 15; tel: 296 216 666; www.pivovarskydum.com; daily 11am–11.30pm; €
This microbrewery and restaurant is noted for its wide and varied range of beers brewed on the premises (even including coffee and banana beer). The hearty Czech food (such as roast pork and stuffed dumplings) is tasty and helps to soak up the drink. Among the other offerings are wheat beer, mead and a delicious dark beer.

Renommé

Na struze 1; tel: 224 934 109; www.renomme.cz; daily 11am–11pm; €€
A small family restaurant offering French food, confit of duck with bacon, dumplings and thyme, foie gras and good soups. Homemade vanilla crème brûlée and chocolate fondant with apple and cinnamon are also highly recommended. Booking is advised.

Triton

Václavské náměstě 26; tel: 221 081 218; www.tritonrestaurant.com; daily 11.30am–11pm; €€€

Enjoy a romantic candlelight dinner in the unique atmosphere of what appears to be a stalactite grotto. Situated in the Adria Hotel's ancient cellars, Triton offers a creative fine dining experience prepared by renowned Chef Michael Novák.

Universal

V Jirchářích 6; tel: 224 934 416; www.universalrestaurant.cz; daily 11.30am–1am; €€
This is a well-priced, comfortable French bistro serving good food. Once settled in the slick interior, you can choose from dishes such as meal-sized salade Niçoise, steaks, and some classic desserts.

U Fleků

Křemencova 11; tel: 224 934 019; www.ufleku.cz; daily 10am–11pm; €€
An ancient and well-known brewery with an illustrious past. Its present is not so glorious, filled as it is with hordes of tourists who bash tables, scoff down plates of goulash and quaff beer. However, the dark beer, brewed on site, is just as wonderful as ever.

U Pinkasů

Jungmannova 16; tel: 221 1111 152; www.upinkasu.cz; daily 10am–11.30pm; €€
While the ground floor and basement of this traditional establishment are given over to rather serious drinkers of Plzeňský prazdroj (on tap here since

The wood-beamed U Bílé Krávy

1843), the more genteel upper floor is an attractive restaurant serving a range of authentic Bohemian dishes.

Vinohrady and Zižkov

Hlučná samota

Záhřebská 14, Vinohrady; tel: 222 522 839; www.hlucna-samota.cz; Mon–Sat 11am–midnight, Sat–Sun noon–midnight; €€

Situated a few blocks down Belgická from náměstí Míru, this pub-cum-restaurant guarantees a convivial atmosphere every evening. As well as serving excellent beer, the menu comprises Czech culinary stalwarts such as beef goulash with dumplings alongside a good selection of lighter dishes that includes salads and vegetarian options.

Orange Moon

Vinohradska 151; tel: 255 742 038; www.orangemoon.cz; daily 11am–10pm; €€

This Thai, Burmese and Indian restaurant is housed in the Atrium Flora shopping gallery. Dishes range from chicken satay and spring rolls to pad thai and fish masala. The food is hot, spicy and tasty.

Pizzeria Grosseto

Francouzská 2/náměstí Míru; tel: 224 252 778; www.grosseto.cz; daily 11.30am–11pm; €

Popular with local residents and office workers, this friendly restaurant serves some of the best pizza in Prague (all freshly cooked in a wood-burning oven). If you enjoy this one you might want to look out for their other branches in Dejvice (Jugoslávských partyzánů 8), Průhonice (Květnové náměstí 11) and Brumlovka (Vyskočilova 2).

Radost FX

Bělehradská 120; tel: 224 254 776; www.radostfx.cz; Mon–Sat 11am–1am, Sun 10.30am–midnight; €

Connected to the eponymous club, this vegetarian restaurant offers a wide range of dishes with influences from the Mediterranean to Mexico to China.

Taverna Olympos

Kubelíkova 9; tel: 222 722 239; www.taverna-olympos.eu; daily 11.30am–11pm; €

Cheerful, popular Greek establishment, with a garden that is a favourite with families. Greek wine as well as tasty Hellenic comestibles.

U Bílé Krávy

Rubešova 10, Vinohrady; tel: 224 239 570; www.bilakrava.cz; Mon–Fri 11.30am–11pm, Sat 5–11pm; €€

Tucked behind the National Museum, the 'White Cow' owes its name to the occupation of its owner, a cattle farmer in Burgundy, France. Most of the dishes use meat from his herd but a variety of seafood and lamb dishes also have their place on the menu. The wood-beamed, cottage-like building has a delightful ambience.

Obecní dům, home to the Prague Symphony Orchestra

NIGHTLIFE

There is something for everyone in Prague, from top-flight classical concerts, to jazz, cinemas and clubs. One of the city's charms is that whatever you are into, you will find the venues relaxed and not as concerned with appearances as might be the case elsewhere.

To purchase tickets it is best to go directly to the box office in order to get the lowest price (and for many places you can book tickets directly online).

Classical Music, Theatre and Ballet

Národní divadlo (National Theatre)
Národní třída 2; tel: 224 901 448;
www.narodni-divadlo.cz
Opera, ballet and theatre performed by the National Theatre ensembles. This is also the location of the Laterna magika 'Black Light' theatre (see page 23).

Obecní dům (Municipal House)
Náměstí Republiky 5; tel: 222 002 101;
www.obecnidum.cz
The splendid Art Nouveau Municipal House has one of the best concert halls in the city and is home to the Prague Symphony Orchestra (www.fok.cz).

The Rudolfinum
Alšovo nábřeží 12/náměstí Jana Palacha;
tel: 227 059 227
This is the home of the Czech Philharmonic (www.ceskafilharmonie.cz) and the Prague Radio Symphony Orchestra (www.rozhlas.cz/socr). The main concert season runs from October to May.

Státní Opera Praha (Prague State Opera)
Wilsonova 4; tel: 224 227 266;
www.opera.cz
Productions here are usually of a very high standard. The repertory offers a mix of 19th-century opera and more daring contemporary works. The Opera is closed for renovation until 2018, see www.narodni-divadlo.cz for alternative venues.

Stavovské divadlo (Estates Theatre)
Ovocný trh 6; tel: 224 901 448;
www.narodni-divadlo.cz
Don Giovanni was premièred here in 1787, conducted by Mozart himself, and his operas are still regularly staged here today. Part of the National Theatre network, the venue also hosts dance and theatre productions.

Jazz Clubs

AghaRTA Jazz Centrum
Železná 16; tel: 222 211 275 (evenings only); www.agharta.cz
This jazz club is popular with all ages and nationalities. It is a good place to catch top local musicians and it organises an ongoing jazz festival, attracting high-quality foreign bands.

The Estates Theatre

Reduta Jazz Club
Národní třída 20; tel: 224 933 487;
www.redutajazzclub.cz
Reduta's something of a legend on the Prague music scene and still going strong. Talent ranges from the old jazz greats and big bands to contemporary modern jazz.

U Malého Glena
Karmelitská 23; tel: 257 531 717;
www.malyglen.cz
Intimate (read tiny) basement that is home to some of the finest jazz in Prague. Good acoustics and a decent bar add to the attractions.

Ungelt Jazz & Blues Club
Týn 2; tel: 224 895 748; www.jazzungelt.cz
Aimed more at visitors than locals, with a cosy stone interior and a casual crowd. It's the only club where you can see the legendary Luboš Andršt Blues Band.

Cinemas

English-language films in Prague are usually shown with Czech subtitles. The following places have more daring selections of new and classic movies: Kino Aero (Biskupcova 31; tel: 271 771 349; www.kinoaero.cz); Evald (Národní třída 28; tel: 221 105 225; www.evald.cz); and MAT Studio (Karlovo náměstí 19; tel: 224 915 765; www.mat.cz).

Nightlife

Karlovy Lázně
Novotného Lávka 5; tel: 739 054 641;
www.karlovylazne.cz

Five floors of hip hop, R'n'B, electronic dance, retro, trance and techno make this one of the most popular nightspots in Prague. Located near the Charles Bridge, it gets thronged with locals and tourists alike, so arrive early, especially at weekends.

Lucerna Music Bar
Vodičkova 36; tel: 224 217 108;
www.musicbar.cz
This large underground club features a themed 1980s and 90s video music club at the weekend. During the week it's a good place to catch live Czech bands.

Mecca
U průhonu 3; tel: 734 155 300;
www.mecca.cz
Large and flash, the Mecca attracts top local DJs and packs club-goers in for its party nights. Jazz nights are courtesy of Jazz Club Železná.

Radost FX
Bělehradská 120; tel: 224 254 776;
www.radostfx.cz
Still the king of dance clubs, with a good crowd and top local and international DJs playing lots of house and R'n'B. Good vegetarian restaurant.

Roxy
Dlouhá 33; tel: 602 691 015; www.roxy.cz
This popular venue presents an eclectic mix of top foreign DJs and contemporary art shows. The music scene here is more hard core than other city venues.

A–Z

A

Age restrictions

The age of consent for heterosexual, gay and lesbian sex is 15 in the Czech Republic. To buy and drink alchohol you must be 18 years old or over; the same restrictions apply for driving a car.

B

Budgeting

Prague offers good value for money for a European city break, but fluctuations in the strength of the crown (koruna) against the pound, dollar and euro are inevitable. Expect to pay from £80–150 ($125–230) a night for a double room in a decent hotel. Eating out has risen in cost, but beer is still cheap, at around Kč80–100 a glass in the city centre, less outside. A taxi into town from the airport will cost from Kč600–1,000, but it is perfectly possible to use public transport (bus then tram or metro): a basic transferable ticket costs Kč32 and a 24-hour ticket costs Kč110 for adults; Kč16 and Kč55 for children aged 6–15 (over the age of 10 proof of age is required).

C

Children

Prague is generally a child-friendly des-

tination, with a number of attractions either aimed at children or that both adults and children will find interesting. Children are usually eligible for reduced rates or even free entry to museums and galleries. Children six to 15 years old have reduced rates on public transport (see Budgeting), and on certain tickets and days can travel free if they are accompanied by a fare-paying adult.

Clothing

Prague has a mild version of the standard Central European climate of cold winters and warm summers. Visitors should pack plenty of warm clothes, including gloves and a hat for the winter, and light clothes for summer. However, the weather can be changeable, so it is advisable to have a light jumper or coat with you in the summer, and to carry an umbrella year round.

If you intend on visiting churches, then to avoid giving offence, you should be modestly dressed with covered shoulders and no shorts or short skirts.

Crime and safety

Prague is a safe, pleasant city to explore on foot. Violent crime is rare, but petty crime – such as car theft and pick-pocketing, especially on tram 22 or on Charles Bridge and in Wenceslas Square – has risen sharply in parallel with the growing number of visitors.

Castle guard

Customs

Travellers within the EU have no limit on the amount of duty free tobacco and alcohol they can bring in for their personal use but customs will seize large amounts if they believe it is for commercial use. Non-EU travellers are allowed to import the following duty-free goods: 200 cigarettes or 100 cigarillos or 50 cigars or 250g of tobacco; 1 litre of spirits; 2 litres of wine; 50ml of perfume or 250ml of eau de Cologne. Gifts are only taxable if the quantity and value are not in keeping with the 'reasonable needs' of the recipient. Other reasonable items are allowed tax free as long as it is for personal use. It is illegal to export antiques without a permit.

If arriving directly from or traveling to a country outside the EU, you must declare any amounts of currency that exceed €10,000 (or the equivalent in another currency). Keep your currency-exchange receipts as you may be required to show them.

Cycling in Prague

Cycling in Prague is gaining in popularity and there is a move towards becoming a more positive cycling city by improving paths and instigating new routes. The A2 cycling route follows the right bank of the river all the way to the suburbs and out into the countryside. There are plenty of opportunities for bike tours and to rent your own bikes. E-bikes (electric bikes) will be popular with those appreciating a little help along the way.

Useful websites and places for cycling rental and tours include: Praha Bike; tel: 732 388 880; www.prahabike.cz; E-bike Prague Rents and Tours; tel: 775 004 078; www.pragueebiketour.cz; Citybike Prague; tel: 776 180 284; www.citybike-prague.com.

Disabled travellers

Prague's public transport was not designed with disabled people in mind. Most metro stations and all trams and buses involve climbing and descending steep steps; although efforts are being made to improve accessibility. Some 65 per cent of buses have wheelchair accessibility but only around 25 per cent of trams. In some cases there is a long wait for the accessible public transport. It may mean people in wheelchairs who wish to use public transport have to be carried bodily on and off trams and buses, and pavement kerbs do not often have ramps.

In general, though, Praguers are courteous to people with disabilities, and will make efforts to assist them. For further information: www.presbariery.cz; www.accessibleprague.com

Electricity

Electricity in the Czech Republic is at AC 220 volts. Two-pin plugs or adaptors are needed for UK appliances with three-pin plugs.

Exhibition Hall detail

Embassies and consulates

Australia: Klimentská 10, Prague 1; tel: 221 729 260.
Canada: Ve Struhách 2, Prague 6; tel: 272 101 800; www.canada.cz.
Ireland: Tržiště 13, Prague 1; tel: 257 530 061; www.embassyofireland.cz..
New Zealand: Vaclavske Namesti 11, Prague 1; tel: 234 784 777.
South Africa: Ruská 65, Prague 10; tel: 267 311 114; www.saprague.cz.
UK: Thunovská 14, Prague 1; tel: 257 402 111.
US: Tržiště 15, Prague 1; tel: 257 022 000; www.usembassy.cz.

Emergencies

General emergency: tel: 112
Ambulance: tel: 155
Fire brigade: tel: 150
Police: tel: 158
Emergency road service: tel: 1230/ 1240

Lost or stolen credit cards
American Express; tel: 222 800 111
Visa/Eurocard; tel: 800-142-121
Mastercard; tel: 800-142-494
Diner's Club; tel: 255 712 712

Etiquette

Generally speaking the Czechs are easy-going and very hospitable. However, they are not terribly impressed (understandably) with the hordes of stag and hen parties that descend on their capital and cause mayhem. The British in particular have a bad reputation for getting drunk and getting into trouble, even though the vast majority of visitors are usually sober and well behaved.

Respect local sensibilities: when visiting a place of worship, dress modestly and do not expose too much flesh.

Festivals

March
One World
A film festival of documentaries that focus on human rights. www.oneworld.cz

March–April
Febio Fest
The largest international film festival in Central Europe. www.febiofest.cz

April
Days of European Film
A festival split between the cities of Prague and Brno, with diverse offerings from the European film industry. www.eurofilmfest.cz

May
Czech Beer Festival Prague
A two-week festival featuring more than 70 brands of Czech beer, complemented by the best of Czech food.

May–June
Khamoro
An annual festival of Roma culture with

Letna Park

music and seminars. www.khamoro.cz

Prague Spring

This prestigious international music festival features concerts at the Rudolfinum, Obecní dům and St Vitus's Cathedral. www.festival.cz

Prague Fringe Festival

A cultural exchange on a vast scale, in which performing artists from dozens of countries meet in Prague to perform everything from puppetry to classical theatre and musical cabaret. www.praguefringe.com

June

Prague Writers' Festival

This meeting of the minds draws some of the top scribes in the world. Past events were hosted by the authors J.M. Coetzee, Salman Rushdie and Gore Vidal. www.pwf.cz

Tanec Praha

A wonderfully diverse celebration of modern dance. www.tanecpha.cz

September–October

4+4 Days in Motion

An international festival of contemporary art featuring theatre, dance, fine art, music and film.
www.ctyridny.cz

October–November

International Jazz Festival

This is one of the oldest jazz festivals in Europe. Many performances are held in the Reduta Jazz Club, considered one of the top ten clubs in Europe.

November–May

Agharta Prague Jazz Festival

A bit of a misnomer, since this 'festival' is actually a series of high-quality concerts, usually one a month, from autumn to spring. Concerts are usually held at Lucerna Music Bar. Performers in recent years have included the Pat Metheny Group and saxophonist Candy Dulfer. www.agharta.cz

December

Miklaus (St Nicholas) Day

Every 5 December the Christmas season begins with St Nicholas roaming the streets with a devil and an angel handing out sweets.

Gay and lesbian issues

Prague is generally very safe – though not necessarily out and proud – for gays and lesbians, and most people will encounter few problems. An excellent site for up-to-date information can be found at www.prague.gayguide.net. The main lesbian site (in Czech) is www.lesba.cz.

Green issues

Large parts of the Czech Republic suffered from severe pollution from Communist-era heavy industry. Air pollution overall, however, has decreased by 50 percent since the 1980s, but there is still a long way to go. Stricter controls imposed by conditions of entry into the EU are already starting to have an effect.

The Theological Hall in the Strahov Monastery

Being situated between hills means air can become trapped in Prague, making winter smog more likely; a report by the Organisation for Economic Cooperation and Development (OECD) revealed that the amount of nitrogen oxide in Prague is well above the EU and OECD average; a rapid increase in traffic levels in Prague since the 1989 revolution has exacerbated the pollution problem. In 2016 Prague was targeted as not meeting the EU pollution requirements and was told that further action needed to be taken.

Carbon offsetting

Air travel produces a huge amount of carbon dioxide and is a significant contributor to global warming. If you would like to offset the damage caused to the environment by your flight, a number of organisations can do this for you, using online 'carbon calculators', which tell you how much you need to donate.

In the UK travellers can visit www.climatecare.org or www.carbonneutral.com; in the US log on to www.climatefriendly.com or www.sustainabletravel.org.

H

Health

Visiting the Czech Republic poses no major health concerns and you do not need any inoculations. Citizens of EU countries, including the UK are enti-tled to free emergency treatment. Make sure you have a European Health Insurance Card before travelling. However, this does not cover all eventualities, so it makes sense to take out adequate health and accident insurance.

A number of medical facilities with English-speaking medical personnel cater specifically to visitors. For minor health problems, Prague has plenty of modern pharmacies (look for a green cross, or the word *lékárna* on the front of the shop), including 24-hour facilities at Palackého 5 and Belgická 37.

The Na Homolce Hospital for for-eigners is located at Roentgenova 2, Prague 5; tel: 257 273 289; www.homolka.cz. For first aid visit Health Center Prague at Vodičkova 28, Prague 2; tel: 224 220 040; 24-hour call line tel: 603 433 833.

For dental emergencies: Palackého 5, Prague 1; tel: 224 946 981.

Holidays

1 January: New Year's Day
Good Friday: variable
Easter Monday: variable
1 May: May Day (Labour Day)
8 May: Day of Liberation from Fascism
5 July: Feast Day of SS Cyril and Methodius
6 July: Anniversary of Jan Hus's death
28 September: St Wenceslas Day
28 October: Day of the origin of the independent Czechoslovakia
17 November: Day of Students' Struggle for Democracy, commemorating the

Street art

Velvet Revolution
25–26 December: Christmas

I

Internet facilities

Many shopping malls, restaurants, pubs, bars and cafés in central Prague have internet access. It is likely that your hotel will have internet facilities and possibly also Wi-fi in your room.

L

Language

The national language is Czech. However, English is widely spoken, as is German. If you can learn a few Czech words, it will always be appreciated. For a language glossary see page 132.

Lost property

To see if your lost property has been handed in contact the office at Karolíny Svě tlé 5, Prague 1; tel: 224 235 085; Mon, Wed 8am–5.30pm, Tue, Thu 8am–4pm, Fri 8am–2pm (closed for lunch noon–12.30pm).

M

Maps

Free maps are available from tourist information offices (see page 128). We also recommend *Insight Fleximap Prague*, a durable and waterproof map with information of the city's top attractions as well as practical information.

Media

Television and radio

Satellite television has one or more English-speaking news channels. The main ones are CNN and BBC 24. Foreign broadcasts on Czech television are dubbed rather than subtitled, although there may be English-speaking programmes on other foreign-service television stations.

Radio Praha broadcasts news in English several times a day. It is only possible to listen via the internet or on your mobile; for further information check www.radio.cz.

Press

All the main foreign-language newspapers are available at news-stands in the city. There are also several English publications printed locally and aimed at visitors to the city. A good resource is *Prague in Your Pocket*, a bimonthly publication highlighting various cultural events around the city. It also includes information on shopping, hotels and cultural festivals and can also be downloaded online (www.inyourpocket.com/prague). The Prague Daily Monitor (www.praguemonitor.com) is an online English-language newspaper aimed mostly at the expat community.

Money

The currency of the Czech Republic is the crown or koruna (Kč). Each crown is made up of 100 hellers (hal.). There are 5,000Kč, 2,000Kč, 1,000Kč, 500Kč,

Memorial to the victims of Communism

200Kč, 100Kč, notes; and coins of 50Kč, 20Kč, 10Kč, 5Kč, 2Kč, 1Kč.

Some items may still be priced in hellers but they are always rounded up to the nearest crown.

Exchange

There are numerous banks and bureaux de change in the city. Banks are open from 8/9am to 4/5pm, but some close for an hour or two at lunch time. Most charge a standard commission of around 2 percent. Bureaux de change have much more flexible hours, often remaining open until 10pm, but they can charge up to 30 percent commission, so it pays to shop around. Some offer 0 percent commission but may offer lower rates. Hotels will also change currency but their commission rates are rarely competitive.

If you want to exchange any crowns you have left back to your own currency before you leave the Czech Republic, you must have an official receipt for your original currency exchange.

Credit cards, ATMs and traveller's cheques

Credit cards are increasingly accepted for payment across the city. They are now accepted by most hotels, but it is still wise to double-check before paying in a restaurant or a shop.

Many cashpoints will issue cash against your current account card or credit card; this is generally the easiest way to get money.

Traveller's cheques offer a safe way of carrying cash and can be exchanged at banks, but stick to the major issuers. Note that they will not be accepted as payment in shops, restaurants or hotels.

Tipping

Tipping is appreciated, but levels are low, and in some restaurants service is included in the price – it should state this on the menu.

Opening hours

Grocery shops open Monday–Friday 7am–6pm, with other shops open 10am–6pm, although those in the centre catering to the tourist trade often remain open late year-round. Smaller shops may close for a couple of hours for lunch. On Saturday, most shops outside the centre close at noon or 1pm, but shops in the centre, especially large department stores, may retain weekday hours on Saturday and Sunday as well. The main commercial streets with dependably long hours year-round are Wenceslas Square and Na příkopě.

Police

State police are responsible for day-to-day policing. They wear white shirts and dark-grey trousers or skirts. They are armed. Municipal police wear light-grey trousers or skirts. Traffic police are responsible for all road and traffic regulations.

SS Peter and Paul Church

Post

Postal services are cheap and reliable for letters and postcards. Most shops that sell postcards also sell stamps, as do many hotels. Postboxes are either orange with a side slit or orange-and-blue with a front flap.

The main post office (2am–midnight) is at Jindřišská 14, off Wenceslas Square. Here you can send telegrams, make international calls, and buy stamps and phonecards. Rates for letters and postcards change periodically. For more information see www.ceskaposta.cz.

Religion

Generally speaking the Czechs are suspicious of organised religion (only 20 percent of the population professes to believe in God) and the country is a secular republic. However, the dominant religion historically and with the largest number of believers is Catholicism.

There are many Jewish visitors to Prague, who come in search of its impressive Jewish heritage. For more information see www.kehilaprag.cz/en.

S

Smoking

The only places free from tobacco smoke seem to be hospitals and public transport; otherwise, the Czechs light up everywhere.

T

Telephones

The international code for the Czech Republic is 420. The city code for Prague is 2, but this is included in the nine-digit number so should not be dialled in addition. Most phone numbers consist of nine digits, including the area code. Dial the entire nine-digit number even if you are dialling within the same area code. If you have problems getting through to a number, call Prague directory enquiries on 1180. Public telephones take phonecards (*telefonní karta*). These can be bought at post offices or news-stands.

Mobile phones

Most people will find that their own mobile (cell) phones work in Prague (even if the charges will be much higher than for using phonecards). However, for longer stays it is better and much cheaper to buy a local pay-as-you-go SIM card. The main local providers are O2 (www.o2.cz/osobni/en/) and Vodafone (www.vodafone.cz).

Time zones

Prague operates on Central European Time (CET). This is one hour ahead of GMT in winter and two hours ahead of GMT in summer.

Toilets

There are public toilets at each metro station, which should stay open until

Transport from bygone times at the Transport Museum

9pm. There is usually a small fee of around 5–10Kč. Public toilets are free in museums, galleries and concert halls.

If there are no male or female symbols to help you, women's toilets are labelled *Ženy* or *Dámy*, men's are *Muži* or *Páni*.

Tourist information

Prague City Tourism (Staroměstské náměstí 1; www.prague.eu) can provide lots of useful information, including city maps and and addresses.

As well as at the main address above, branches can be found at: crossroads of Na Můsktu/Rytířská, Staré Město; Václavské náměstí, Nové Město (all three open daily 9am–7pm); Terminal 1 and 2, Václav Havel Airport (both open daily 8am–8pm).

Tours

Prague offers a wide range of excellent tours covering topics ranging from underground passages, ghosts, and beer to World War II and life under Communism, and involve various ways of getting around:

Sandemans New Prague Tours (www.neweuropetours.eu/prague; daily 10am, 10.45am, noon, 2pm). An excellent free introductory walking tour to Prague led by a local. Book online or meet at Old Town Square (Staroměstské náměstí). Other tours (charge) are also available.

Ghosts and Legends Tour (tel: 608 200 912; www.prague-ghost-tour.com; daily Apr–Sept 8.30pm, 10pm, Nov–Mar 7pm, 8.30pm). Let your costumed guide take you through the most haunted areas and hear the grizzly medieval tales.

Old Town and Underground (tel: 608 200 912; www.prague-underground-tours.com; daily 11am, 1pm, 5pm, also 3pm June–Sept). Under the city are a wealth of medieval passages and cellars. Evening tours are also available. Tours start at the ticket office at Malé náměstí 11.

Vintage car tours: Explore Prague in a replica vintage car from c1930s/40s. With a knowledgeable guide at the wheel, you can customise your trip. For information: Prague History Trip (www.historytrip.cz); 3 Veteráni (www.3veterani.cz).

Boat tours: Several operators run boat trips down the Vltava and most leave from the embankment just below Čechův most (the Czech bridge) near the Hotel Continental. They run year-round but are more frequent in the summer. For more information: EVD (www.evd.cz); Prague Boats (www.prague-boats.cz) and Cruise Prague (www.cruise-prague.cz).

Transport

Prague Airport

Prague's expanded and modernised, Václav Havel Airport located at Ruzyně lies about 20km (13 miles) northwest of the city. For flight information tel: 220 111 888 or check www.prg.aero. It is possible to book a flight to Prague from most European capitals and from New York, Montreal and Toronto. The flight from London takes about two hours. The national airline is čsa (České Aeroline; www.csa.cz).

Numerous budget airlines now fly to Prague. From the UK these include: easyJet (www.easyjet.com), flying from Gatwick, Stansted, Bristol, Manchester and Edinburgh; RyanAir (www.ryanair.com) flying from Stansted and Liverpool; and Jet2 (www.jet2.com) with flights from Glasgow, Newcastle, East Midlands, Leeds-Bradford and Manchester. The Czech-based Smart Wings (www.smartwings.net) flies from Amsterdam, Barcelona, Dubai, Madrid, Paris, Rome and Valencia among other cities.

The Czech airline ČSA (www.csa.cz) flies direct from Toronto to Prague; Delta airlines fly direct from New York. For visitors coming from other starting points in Canada or the US, it might make more sense to fly direct to London and then connect with a flight on one of the carriers listed above.

Transport from the airport

The cheapest way into the city from the airport (or vice versa) is by city transport. The public bus service 119 reaches the new metro station at Nádraží Veleslavín (Line A), probably the most useful for the majority of visitors and the metro at Zličín is reached by bus 100. The journey by bus 119 takes about 17 minutes; 15 minutes by bus 100 and tickets are available from either the DPP counter in the arrivals hall or from machines by the bus stop just outside the terminal building. If you arrive late at night, a night bus (510) will take you to the tram stop at Divoká Šárka, where you can pick up the night tram (51) into town.

The Airport Express bus (AE bus) connects the airport with the main railway station Praha Hlavni Nadrazi, where there is a connection to metro line C; travel time is 35 minutes and the ticket can be bought from the driver.

A private minibus shuttle service, Čedaz (tel: 220 114 296; www.cedaz.cz), operates between the airport and V Celnici, close to náměstí Republiky, every half-hour from 7.30am to 7pm. The journey between the airport and the náměstí Republiky terminus takes 30–45 minutes and costs around 150Kč. They also have a number of minibuses that will take you directly to your hotel for a fee. However, the rates for these are almost as high as taxi fares.

Several taxi companies operate from the airport into town. Taxis are lined up outside the arrivals exit. Rates are relatively high, however; a ride to the centre generally costs about 650Kč. Companies include: **Fix Taxis** (tel: 220 113 892) with stands outside Terminals 1 and 2, easily recognised by their yellow metred taxis and **Taxi Praha** (tel: 222 111 000). **Prague Airport Transfers** (tel: 222 554 211; www.prague-airport-transfers.co.uk) are a pre-book or call on arrival service with a car promised within 10 minutes; prices from 550Kč (see also Taxis, below).

By train

The most direct way to reach Prague from London by train is via Paris and Frankfurt, which takes around 18 hours (for details and booking check www.raileurope.co.uk). Some of these trains arrive at Smíchov.

Heading down into the metro

Public transport

Prague has a comprehensive and integrated public-transport system that provides a cheap and efficient service (www.dpp.cz). The extremely efficient Prague metro opened in 1974 and provides a great service for visitors. There are three interlinked lines (construction starts on a fourth line (D) in 2018), and metro maps can be found at each station. Metro signs above ground feature a stylised M incorporated into an arrow pointing downwards. Metro trains operate until midnight.

Buses tend to provide a service out to the Prague suburbs rather than compete with trams in the city.

Tickets and passes can be used on all forms of transport. Each ticket has a time limit, and you obviously pay more for a longer limit. The cheapest ticket costs Kč24 and allows a single trip of 30 minutes' travel, including transfers between lines and types of transport. A Kč32 ticket allows 90 minutes' travel on the same basis. Children aged between six and 15 pay half price.

Tickets can be bought at metro stations (there are automatic ticket machines that give instructions in English and supply change) or newsstands. They must be validated in the small yellow machines you will see when you catch the tram or arrive at the metro station.

Day tickets or longer passes are also available and are valid for unlimited travel on all forms of transport. These can often be supplied by your hotel concierge but can also be purchased at the MHD kiosks at all major metro stations. They will be valid from the date stamped on them and do not have to be validated for each journey. Prices are as follows: 24-hour pass Kč110; three-day pass Kč310; and monthly pass Kč550.

There is a comprehensive network of 31 tram routes, which connects both sides of the river. Each tram stop shows the tram number passing there, and a timetable. Most city maps show the tram routes in addition to the location of the major attractions. All trams run from 4.30am–midnight, but a number of routes are also designated as night routes and operate a service 24 hours a day. Purchase your ticket before you travel and validate it as you enter unless you are transferring from another tram or metro within your allotted time.

On way to cross the River Vltava is by ferry, used by commuters, locals and visitors alike and part of the integrated public transport system. There are six ferry routes; more information on www.ropid.cz/en/ferries.

In addition Prague boasts one nostalgic tram route. Every weekend (Apr–mid-Nov noon–5pm) the historic Tram 91 runs along a city-centre route, taking in a number of sights. The route varies but generally runs from the museum to the Výstaviště exhibition ground via Malá Strana, the National Theatre, Wenceslas Square and Náměstí republicky. The trip takes about 40 minutes, leaving on the hour, and returns to the museum (see www.dpp.cz).

Tram rails

Taxis

There are some unscrupulous operators, and overcharging is a common complaint. Phoning for a taxi is cheaper than hailing one, as rates are lower and you won't be overcharged. Two reputable firms with staff who speak English are **Taxi Praha** (tel: 222 111 000; www.taxi-praha.cz) and **Profi Taxi** (tel: 140 15; www.profitaxi.cz).

If you must hail a taxi, check the rates listed on the passenger door against the meter, or negotiate a price beforehand; a journey in the city centre should not cost more than Kč100–200; a trip to or from the airport generally cots about Kč650.

Driving

Even for drivers who know Prague, the city can be a traffic nightmare. Large sections of Staré Město and Malá Strana have been completely closed to traffic. If you do manage to get through the maze of one-way streets and culs-de-sac to find yourself in the centre you will probably be turned away by the police (or may even get a ticket) unless you can prove you are resident at one of the hotels nearby. It is therefore highly advisable to leave your car at home and explore the city either on foot or by public transport.

V

Visas and passports

Citizens of the European Union (EU) – of which the Czech Republic is a member – and of most other European countries need only a passport to visit the Czech Republic for up to 90 days. Citizens of the US, Canada, New Zealand and Australia can also stay for up to 90 days with just a passport. Citizens of South Africa can enter the Czech Republic but must first obtain a visa. Passports from EU visitors need only be valid for the length of stay but they must not expire before leaving the Czech Republic. All other passports must be valid for at least 90 days from the date of your arrival in the Czech Republic.

Websites

Useful websites include:
www.czechtourism.com (the main Czech tourism authority);
www.dpp.cz (Prague public transport);
www.prague.eu (Prague City Tourism);
www.pragueexperience.com (online guide with a wealth of information).

Weights and measures

The Czech Republic uses the metric system of measurement.

Women travellers

Although feminism still has a long way to go in the Czech Republic, women travelling in Prague and the rest of the Czech Republic should not expect to encounter any particular problems. If you are out by yourself late at night, however, the usual rules of common sense apply. Bear in mind also that pubs in Prague can be very male-dominated environments, and women on their own may not feel comfortable in them.

Kafka Square

LANGUAGE

For native English-speakers Czech appears to have an impenetrable vocabulary, a formidable array of accents and a complex grammar involving bewildering changes in the ending of words. Local people will not expect you to have mastered their language, but as in every country, they will be pleased if you have made the effort to acquire a few basics. One plus point is that Czech, unlike English, is pronounced exactly as it looks. A few – very few – words in international use can be deciphered; examples include *tramvaj* (tramway or tram), *recepce* (hotel reception) and *auto* (car).

Basic Communication

Good morning/how do you do? *Dobřden*
Good evening *Dobř večer*
Good night *Dobrou noc*
Hello *Ahoj*
Goodbye *Na shledanou*
Yes *Ano*
No *Ne*
Please *Prosím*
Thank you *Děkuji*
Excuse me *Promiňte*
I'm sorry *Je mi líto*
How are you? *Jak se máte?* (This may be interpreted literally)
Fine, thanks *Děkuji, dobře*
And you? *A vy?*
Cheers! (when drinking) *Na zdraví!*
Help! *Pomoc!*
I am looking for... *Hledám...*

What? *Co?*
Where? *Kde?*
Where is/are? *Kde je/jsou?*
When? *Kdy?*
How? *Jak?*
How much? *Kolik?*
How much does it cost? *Kolik to stojí?*
I want *Chci*
We want *Chceme*
I would like *Chtěl bych* (*chtěla bych* if the speaker is female)
I don't know *Nevím*
I don't understand *Nerozumím*
Slowly, please! *Pomalu, prosím!*
Here *Tady*
There *Tam*

Numbers

0 *nula*
1 *jeden, jedna (feminine), jedno (neuter)*
2 *dva, dvě (feminine, neuter)*
3 *tři*
4 *čtyři*
5 *pět*
6 *šest*
7 *sedm*
8 *osm*
9 *devět*
10 *deset*
11 *jedenáct*
12 *dvanáct*
13 *třináct*
14 *čtrnáct*
15 *patnáct*
16 *šestnáct*

Information signs

17 sedmnáct
18 osmnáct
19 devatenáct
20 dvacet
21 dvacet jeden (or jednadvacet)
22 dvacet dva (or dvaadvacet)
30 třicet
40 čtyřicet
50 padesát
60 šedesát
70 sedmdesát
80 osmdesát
90 devadesát
100 sto
200 dvě stě
300 tři sta
400 čtyři sta
500 pět set
600 šest set
1,000 tisíc

1,000,000 milión
A pair/few pár
Half pěl

Monday pondělí
Tuesday úterý
Wednesday středa
Thursday čtvrtek
Friday pátek
Saturday sobota
Sunday neděle
January leden
February únor
March březen
April duben
May květen
June červen
July červenec
August srpen
September září
October říjen
November listopad
December prosinec
Day den
Morning ráno
Afternoon odpoledne
Evening večer
Night noc
Yesterday včera
Today dnes
Tomorrow zítra
Now teì
What is the time? Kolik je hodin?
One o'clock jedna hodina
Two/three/four o'clock dvě/tři/čtyři hodiny
Five o'clock pět hodin

Helpful signs

Franz Kafka commemorative plaque

BOOKS AND FILM

Since the collapse of Communism and the Velvet Revolution of 1989 a vibrant cultural scene and well-funded arts programme has emerged in the Czech Republic, with Prague at its heart. In 2014 the city was awarded the ninth Unesco City of Literature for its outstanding literary heritage, a dynamic contemporary scene and actively growing investment and international collaboration. This is evident in its roots with the works of Kafka, and his friend and biographer Max Bod; Holocaust survivor and Pulitzer Prize nominee Arnost Lustig; Václav Havel, the playwright, author and president of post-revolution Czechoslovakia and modern Czech writers such as former dissident Jáchym Topol.

There is a long and proud tradition of Czech cinema in a wide genre including drama, comedy and animation. Early cinema flourished after World War I and during the 1920s and 1930s popular Czech films began reaching audiences abroad. The Czech new wave or golden age of cinema evolved from the artistic movement of the 1930s and is centred on the years 1963–1968 when anti-Communist emotions were riding high. Post-Communism brought a falling off in funding and an increase in foreign film production within the country, attracted by low costs and beautiful locations. However in the 1990s a new generation of Czech film makers came to the fore, winning awards

and Oscar nominations. With the support of FAMU (Film and Television School of the Academy of Performing Arts) it is hoped that Czech cinema will continue to flourish.

Books

Non-Fiction

My Crazy Century by Ivan Klíma. The acclaimed dissident novelist's autobiography spans six decades of life in the Czech Republic from boyhood in the Terezin concentration camp, through Communism and eventual liberation and democracy.

Cities of the Imagination – Prague by Richard Burton. A 'cultural and literary history' that gets beneath the skin of the city. Burton's discussions of key figures and events – from Jan Hus, alchemy and the Golem to Kafka, Hašek and the Velvet Revolution – are insightful.

Franz Kafka: a Biography by Max Brod. The classic account of Kafka's life by his lifelong friend and editor.

Magic Prague by Angelo Maria Ripellino. More deftly than any other writer, Ripellino conjures up the esoteric ambience of the city in which strangeness was the norm, from the days of Rabbi Löw and Emperor Rudolf onwards.

We the People by Timothy Garton Ash. Eyewitness account of the thrilling events of late 1989. British journalist and academic Garton Ash was present in the smoke-filled Laterna Magika thea-

Toby Jones in 'Anthropoid'

tre as students and dissidents prepared the peaceful overthrow of Communism.
Under a Cruel Star: A Life in Prague 1941–1968 by Heda Margoloius Kovaly. The intimate and poignant memoir of a woman's life through concentration camps, post-war starvation and her husband's execution in the Stalin purges.

Fiction

The Good Soldier Švejk and His Fortunes in the World War by Jaroslav Hašek, translated by Cecil Parrott. While some prefer the pre-war, anonymous translation into English of the adventures of Hašek's iconic anti-hero, this version by a former British ambassador is totally complete, omitting none of the beery conscript's many expletives and less-than-savoury exploits.

The Golem by Gustav Meyrink. Written in 1913, this book tells of the legend of Rabbi Löw's clay homunculus.

Prague Tales by Jan Neruda (various editions). Charming short stories from the backstreets of the 19th-century city by the 'Dickens of Malá Strana'.

The Trial, The Castle, Metamorphosis and Other Stories by Franz Kafka. Kafka's creation of shadowy worlds in which people are helpless in the face of an unfathomable authority was eerily prophetic of the atmosphere of Prague when it was in the grip of the totalitarian rule first of the Nazis, then the Communists. Despite the enthusiasm of today's tourist industry for this image, the contemporary city seems to have little left of the sinister character so tellingly evoked in Kafka's work.

Film

Films have been made at the Barrandov Studios in southern Prague since 1932, and in their first decade up to 80 films a year were made. During World War II, the studios were confiscated by the Nazis, who exploited the facilities to make propaganda films. After the war, the studios were nationalised and remained under state ownership until the 1990s.

In their desire for cultural and expressive freedom directors such as Jan Němec, Miloš Forman, Klos and Ján Kadár and Jiří Menzel, achieved international acclaim. Films such as *Closely Watched Trains* (Jiří Menzel, 1966) and *The Shop on Main Street* (Klos and Ján Kadár, 1965) won Oscars and Miloš Forman's *The Firemen's Ball* (1967) and *Loves of a Blonde* (1965) were nominated.

After the Soviet clampdown in 1968, many directors chose to emigrate and established themselves abroad. After the Velvet Revolution, difficulties in adapting to the free market nearly led to the studios' bankruptcy in 2000. However, the dramatic decline in the number of Czech films, which are now seeing something of a revival, was gradually compensated for by the increase in foreign productions, particularly those made by US producers, including such blockbusters as *Mission Impossible* (1996), *The Bourne Identity* (2002) and *Casino Royale* (2006). The 2016 World War II thriller *Anthropoid* starring Cillian Murphy and Toby Jones was shot almost entirely in Prague.

ABOUT THIS BOOK

This *Explore Guide* has been produced by the editors of Insight Guides, whose books have set the standard for visual travel guides since 1970. With top-quality photography and authoritative recommendations, these guidebooks bring you the very best routes and itineraries in the world's most exciting destinations.

BEST ROUTES

The routes in the book provide something to suit all budgets, tastes and trip lengths. As well as covering the destination's many classic attractions, the itineraries track lesser-known sights, and there are also excursions for those who want to extend their visit outside the city. The routes embrace a range of interests, so whether you are an art fan, a gourmet, a history buff or have kids to entertain, you will find an option to suit.

We recommend reading the whole of a route before setting out. This should help you to familiarise yourself with it and enable you to plan where to stop for refreshments – options are shown in the 'Food and Drink' box at the end of each tour.

For our pick of the tours by theme, consult Recommended Routes for… (see pages 6–7).

INTRODUCTION

The routes are set in context by this introductory section, giving an overview of the destination to set the scene, plus background information on food and drink, shopping and more, while a succinct history timeline highlights the key events over the centuries.

DIRECTORY

Also supporting the routes is a Directory chapter, with a clearly organised A–Z of practical information, our pick of where to stay while you are there and select restaurant listings; these eateries complement the more low-key cafés and restaurants that feature within the routes and are intended to offer a wider choice for evening dining. Also included here are some nightlife listings, plus a handy language guide and our recommendations for books and films about the destination.

ABOUT THE AUTHORS

This Insight Guides Explore: Prague was written by Maria Lord and Michael Macaroon, both editors and writers specialising in Prague and co-authors of *Smart Guide Prague*. Insight regulars Jackie Staddon and Hilary Weston also contributed to this edition.

CONTACT THE EDITORS

We hope you find this Explore Guide useful, interesting and a pleasure to read. If you have any questions or feedback on the text, pictures or maps, please do let us know. If you have noticed any errors or outdated facts, or have suggestions for places to include on the routes, we would be delighted to hear from you. Please drop us an email at hello@insightguides.com. Thanks!

CREDITS

Explore Prague
Editor: Carine Tracanelli
Authors: Alfred Horn, Maria Lord, Michael Macaroon, Jackie Staddon, Hilary Weston
Head of Production: Rebeka Davies
Update Production: AM Services
Picture Editor: Tom Smyth
Cartography: original cartography Apa Cartography Department, updated by Carte
Photo credits: Alamy 71, 135; Bílá kráva 117; Carlson Rezidor Hotel Group 100ML, 114B; Czech Tourism 28/29; Elan Fleisher/REX/Shutterstock 21; Four Seasons Hotels 100MC, 100MR, 100MR, 100ML, 105T, 111; Getty Images 4/5T, 6MC, 6ML, 7T, 8/9T, 19, 24, 25, 41, 51, 85, 93L, 100/101T, 119, 134; Isifa Image Service sro/REX/Shutterstock 68; iStock 4ML, 4MC, 4MR, 4MR, 4ML, 7MR, 7MR, 8MR, 11L, 12, 12/13, 14/15, 20, 26ML, 26MR, 26ML, 26MC, 26MR, 28, 29L, 34, 47L, 47, 48, 49, 53, 55L, 56, 57L, 58B, 64, 65, 69T, 69B, 97; Leonardo 4MC, 102, 103, 109, 115T; Libor Svacek/Adria – Neptun 116; Mandarin Oriental 104, 105B; Martin Divíšek/Národní divadlo 8MC, 23L; Obecní dům, a.s. 7M, 8ML, 26MC, 100MC, 112, 113, 118; Olivia Rutherford/REX/Shutterstock 63; Pete Bennett/Apa Publications 33; Petr Našic/Národní divadlo 22; Petr Neubert/Národní divadlo 23; Rod Purcell/Apa Publications 1, 30, 31L, 31, 33L, 36, 37, 42L, 43, 43, 52, 54, 55, 57, 58T, 59, 60, 61, 62, 65L, 72, 73, 74, 75, 76, 77L, 77, 78, 80, 93, 95, 98, 99, 120, 121, 122, 123, 124, 125, 126, 127, 128, 129, 130, 131, 132, 133B, 133T; Shutterstock 6TL, 6BC, 8ML, 8MC, 8MR, 10, 11, 16, 17L, 17, 27T, 32, 35, 38, 39L, 39, 44, 45, 46, 53L, 66, 67, 70, 73L, 75L, 79, 81L, 81, 82, 83L, 83, 84, 87, 88, 89, 90, 91L, 91, 92, 94, 96; Terasa U Zlate Studne 110; Vienna House Company 106, 107
Cover: Shutterstock (both)

Printed by CTPS – China

DISTRIBUTION

UK, Ireland and Europe
Apa Publications (UK) Ltd;
sales@insightguides.com
United States and Canada
Ingram Publisher Services;
ips@ingramcontent.com
Australia and New Zealand
Woodslane; info@woodslane.com.au
Southeast Asia
Apa Publications (Singapore) Pte;
singaporeoffice@insightguides.com
Hong Kong, Taiwan and China
Apa Publications (HK) Ltd;
hongkongoffice@insightguides.com
Worldwide
Apa Publications (UK) Ltd;
sales@insightguides.com

SPECIAL SALES, CONTENT LICENSING AND COPUBLISHING

Insight Guides can be purchased in bulk quantities at discounted prices. We can create special editions, personalised jackets and corporate imprints tailored to your needs.
sales@insightguides.com
www.insightguides.biz

INDEX

MAP LEGEND

- ● Start of tour
- ⟶ Tour & route direction
- ❶ Recommended sight
- ❷ Recommended restaurant/café
- ★ Place of interest
- ❶ Tourist information
- Ⓜ Metro station

- 𝑴̂ Museum or gallery
- 𝟏 Statue/monument
- ✉ Main post office
- ☾ Mosque
- 🚌 Main bus station
- ⛴ Ferry station
- ----- Ferry route
- ▬▬ Railway
- ═══ Highway
- ✈ Airport
- ☼ Viewpoint

- ☍ Cave
- ∴ Ancient Site
- 🏰 Castle / castle ruins
- Important building
- Hotel
- Shopping / market
- Pedestrian area
- Urban area
- Park
- National park

INSIGHT ⊙ GUIDES

OFF THE SHELF

Since 1970, INSIGHT GUIDES has provided a unique perspective on the world's best travel destinations by using specially commissioned photography and illuminating text written by local authors.

Whether you're planning a city break, a walking tour or the journey of a lifetime, our superb range of guidebooks and phrasebooks will inspire you to discover more about your chosen destination.

INSIGHT GUIDES

offer a unique combination of stunning photos, absorbing narrative and detailed maps, providing all the inspiration and information you need.

PHRASEBOOKS & DICTIONARIES

help users to feel at home, when away. Pocket-sized with a free app to download, they go where you do.

CITY GUIDES

pack hundreds of great photos into a smaller format with detailed practical information, so you can navigate the world's top cities with confidence.

EXPLORE GUIDES

feature easy-to-follow walks and itineraries in the world's most exciting destinations, with our choice of the best places to eat and drink along the way.

POCKET GUIDES

combine concise information on where to go and what to do in a handy compact format, ideal on the ground. Includes a full-colour, fold-out map.

EXPERIENCE GUIDES

feature offbeat perspectives and secret gems for experienced travellers, with a collection of over 100 ideas for a memorable stay in a city.